START YOUR LIFE
IN *JAPAN*

KEN LAWRENCE

Copyright © 2016 Sailingstone Press LLC

All rights reserved. No part of this publication may be reproduced, distributed, or transmitted in any form or by any means, including photocopying, recording, or other electronic or mechanical methods, without the prior written permission of the publisher, except in the case of brief quotations embodied in critical reviews and certain other noncommercial uses permitted by copyright law.

ISBN-13: 978-0692696972
ISBN-10: 0692696970

Published by Sailingstone Press LLC
690 S Hwy 89, Suite 200
Jackson, WY 83001

Contact: startyourlifeinjapan@gmail.com

Disclaimer: The author has made every effort to ensure the accuracy of the information within this book was correct at time of publication. The author does not assume and hereby disclaims any liability to any party for any loss, damage, or disruption caused by errors or omissions, whether such errors or omissions result from accident, negligence, or any other cause. You are responsible for your own choices, actions, and results.

Table of Contents

Introduction..6
COMING AS A STUDENT OR
THROUGH WORKING HOLIDAY..........................9
    Coming as a High School Student..........................9
    Coming as a University Student............................11
    Japanese Language Schools...................................12
    Working Holiday...14
HUNTING FOR TEACHING JOBS..........................16
    Getting a Teaching Certificate...............................16
    Where to Look for Teaching Jobs Online.............19
    Applying From Abroad..23
    Job Hunting as a Tourist..27
    "How Much Money Should I Bring?"...................29
    Choosing Where to Live..31
    Failing to Find a Job Within 90 Days....................34
THE APPLICATION AND
INTERVIEW PROCESS...36
    Writing Your Resume and Cover Letter................36
    Resume Sample Template.....................................38
    The Interview..41
TEACHING JOB OVERVIEW...................................45
    Teaching English Conversation (Eikaiwa)............45
    Becoming an ALT..47
    The JET Program..49
    Other Kinds of Teaching Jobs...............................52
CELL PHONES, BANK ACCOUNTS
AND OTHER GENERAL INFO.................................59
    Short Term Accommodation.................................59
    Paying Taxes...63
    Getting a Cell Phone..64
    Wifi..66
    Driving in Japan...67

   Setting up a Bank Account......................................69
SURVIVING YOUR TEACHING JOB.....................74
   What's So Bad About Eikaiwa?.............................75
   What's So Bad About Being an ALT?....................81
   The Shakai Hoken Controversy.............................85
   Company Accommodation......................................89
   Joining a Union...90
UNEMPLOYMENT..93
   Quitting Your Job..93
   Collecting Unemployment Insurance....................95
   Living Frugally...99
ALL ABOUT VISAS...101
   Applying For a Visa Before Arrival in Japan.......101
   Applying for a Visa from Within Japan...............102
   Recent Changes to The System............................104
   Renewing Your Visa...106
   Different Types of Visas......................................107
BEYOND TEACHING..118
   Other Career Paths...119
   Headhunting...134
RENTING AN APARTMENT....................................143
   Fees and Useful Terms...143
   Japanese Apartment Types..................................147
   The Process..148
   Discrimination...151
   Cost of Rent...152
   Necessary Documents...153
   Buying Furniture...154
   Who You Will Deal With....................................157
   Garbage Disposal..157
   Furniture Disposal...159
   Avoiding Drama..160
   Contract Renewal..162
SURVIVING EVERYDAY LIFE...............................164

- You Need a Hobby 164
- Japanese Medical Care 166
- Medical Tourism 169
- Bringing Over Prescription Medication 170
- Being Vegetarian in Japan 171
- Racism and Xenophobia 173
- Knowing the Laws 175
- Getting Stopped by The Police 178
- Getting Arrested 183

LEARNING THE LANGUAGE 186
- Reading and Writing 187
- Speaking and Pronunciation 188
- Keigo 190
- Useful Resources 192
- Language, Otherness and Dating 194
- Language and Cultural Defense Mechanisms 195
- Language and Employment 196
- The JLPT 197
- The Usefulness of Japanese 199

UNDERSTANDING THE JAPANESE 201
- It's All About the Wa 201
- Honne and Tatemae 202
- Uchi and Soto 203
- Senpai and Kohai 205
- Giri 206
- Gaman 208
- "Shou ga nai" 209
- Your Place as a Foreigner 209
- Conclusion 212

Introduction

Japan has long captivated Westerners' imaginations for centuries. If you're reading this, chances are there's something about the country and culture that fascinates you. Maybe it's the traditional arts, the food, the natural scenery or the colorful fashion and pop culture. Maybe you even dream of living and working here some day. If so, this book will help you turn that dream into a reality.

This book is meant to be a practical, useful guide for those determined to move to Japan and find work at all costs. This is the book I wished had existed back when I was in your shoes. After finishing university, I knew that I wanted to come back and live in Japan after having spent some time here as a student. But I didn't know how. I was confused and overwhelmed by all the information out there on things like visas and housing and I wasn't sure what kind of job I'd actually be able to get as a foreigner.

After a lot of research, I came to the conclusion that becoming an English teacher would be the quickest way to get my foot in the door here, and I imagine that's also going to be the case for many of you too. I took the leap and came to job hunt as a tourist, barely managing to find a job and a visa before my 90 days ran out. Since then, several years have already flown by. After a few years in the

ESL industry I've worked for a couple of Japanese companies and have even started my own business. Accomplishing my goals in Japan did not come without a struggle, however. Let's face it. Japan is not the most accessible place for foreigners by any means. But if you're willing to put in enough hard work and effort then you can make it here.

In the following pages you'll find information on how to come here as a student, how to hunt for teaching jobs, interview tips and even a resume sample. I also go over how to get a cell phone, a driver's license and open a bank account. Then there's info on unemployment insurance, how to rent your own apartment, details on the different visa categories and a long list of job opportunities outside of the ESL industry. Finally, I talk about staying healthy and out of trouble, the importance of learning the language and an introduction to understanding some fundamental concepts of Japanese culture.

What this book is not:

This book is not a travel guide and it's not intended for anyone just coming here on holiday. Nor is this a Japanese language text book. But I will share a number of study tips and talk about how much of the language you really need to learn. You won't find any translation guides for things like buying a train ticket or figuring out your washing machine, but feel free to email me and I'd be happy to share some useful resources.

Also, understand that this book is **not** an advertisement for Japan. I don't sugarcoat anything about life and work here! I go into detail about some of the darker realities of Japan's work culture and life as a foreigner which may disappoint or discourage you. It's certainly not my intention, however, to dissuade you from coming here. If you're really determined to start a life here then these are things you're going to end up dealing with sooner or later, so please don't shoot the messenger! As you read, keep in mind that even after experiencing a lot of the difficult and stress-inducing topics mentioned in this book, there were still enough good things to keep me here for so long.

I've lived in Japan for around a decade total and throughout my time here I've met loads of amazing people and have so many fantastic and hilarious memories that I could share. But this book is meant to be a practical guide and not a collection of memoirs. As I go into detail on what you need to do to start a life here, some of the grittier, unpleasant or simply mundane aspects of surviving in a new country are going to come up. My ultimate goal is to help you deal with these things as smoothly as possible so that you can focus more time and energy on enjoying this new chapter of your life.

1

COMING AS A STUDENT OR THROUGH WORKING HOLIDAY

Coming to Japan as a student is an excellent way to first get acquainted with the country. You won't need to deal with the pressure of a typical Japanese work environment and you'll have a lot more time and flexibility to travel than someone coming here for work. Studying in Japan will give you a major head start if you do eventually return to look for a job, as you'll already be conversationally fluent, have local connections and a basic understanding of the people and culture. If you're interested in coming straight here for work, feel free to skip ahead to Chapter 2 or to the last section of this chapter on Working Holiday.

Coming as a High School Student

If you're still in high school, there are several youth exchange student programs out there for you to consider. One of the biggest and most well-known programs is Rotary Youth Exchange. Through Rotary you can live in Japan for a year and stay with host families while attending a local public high school. To join the program you'll first need to go through an extensive application and interview process. While not everyone gets in, the acceptance rate is fairly high. If you do get accepted, keep in mind that there's a high chance you'll be sent to a very small town that no one's ever heard of. Even if it's your dream to live in Tokyo some day, it's best to demonstrate flexibility in regards to location during the interview.

It doesn't matter if your family isn't part of the Rotary Club and once you join the program, the local club in your town will be assisting you and cooperating with your new host club in Japan. They'll coordinate to set up things like the host families you'll live with and the high school you'll attend. These are typical Japanese high schools so expect to dress up in a school uniform every day. Since all your classes will be conducted in Japanese, there's little expectation for you to actually complete your assignments or take tests, with the exception of English, math or art. You'll also be encouraged to join an extracurricular club which can be both a culturally enriching experience as well as a good way to make friends.

Staying with a host family will give you an opportunity to experience local holidays and traditional customs. Rotary typically sends students to multiple host families throughout the year, which can be both a good and a bad thing. On the one hand, seeing how different families live will broaden your perspective, but on the other hand, it may be harder to become close with any one particular family. Another major exchange program called AFS sets you up with just one family for the entire year. This means you'll likely form a close bond with them, provided you all get along in the first place. If you don't then you can expect the year to go by very slowly!

Many of these exchange programs, especially Rotary, are quite cheap. It depends on your nationality and which program you choose, but accommodation with your host families and the food they cook for you all year are generally included in the price. If your parents are the ones paying, you can sell them on the program by explaining how they could actually save money by sending you to Japan!

Coming as a University Student

If you're currently in university, check and see if your school has an exchange program that can send you here. This is an easy way to come as a student and since it won't require a major commitment to the country, you'll get a chance to decide if Japan is really for you in the long run.

There are also a number of English-language undergrad programs out there that you may want to consider. If living in Tokyo is your goal, one of the most popular schools is the Japan Campus of Temple University. Other options include Sophia University and Meiji University. And then there are the ultra elite Tokyo University and Waseda, but considering how difficult these are even for Japanese to get into, they may be somewhat of a long shot.

Outside of Tokyo you have options like Kyoto University (another top tier school), Kyoto Seika, Ritsumeikan, and regional schools like Osaka, Tohoku and Hokkaido Universities. Many of these universities have postgraduate programs as well. The web site univinjapan.com is a great resource to learn more about English language university programs around the country.

When applying to a Japanese university you'll have to send in an application form specific to the school of your choice. An application fee is generally required which could cost up to around ¥20,000. Along with your application, include a high school transcript. You may or may not need to get this translated into Japanese first. You'll also need to write an essay explaining why you want to attend that school and how the program could help you reach your goals in the future. When talking about why you want to live in Japan, it's probably a better idea to mention something other than anime or manga. Try writing about a more traditional aspect of the culture that interests you. Obviously, don't hide your passion for manga if you're applying specifically for a manga program at Kyoto Seika University, for example. After sending everything to Japan, you'll hopefully be invited for an interview with an admissions counselor over Skype.

Japanese Language Schools

Another way to get an easy visa to live in Japan would be to enroll in a Japanese language school. There are thousands of language schools around the country so it's best to have a general location in mind first. Language schools have courses available for all kinds of purposes. For example, you could take university or post-graduate prep courses, study for a certain level of the JLPT (Japanese Language Proficiency Test) or just take some basic conversational Japanese lessons.

Most schools have an option to study for three, six or twelve months. The average six-month course at a typical school costs in the range of ¥4 - ¥500,000. Luckily, students in Japan are allowed to get part-time jobs for up to 28 hours per week so you can at least recover some of the costs. Working as a student requires getting a special work permit from the government and the application process can take around 3 weeks. Many exchange students work at convenience stores, supermarkets or at restaurants. It should go without saying that the types of part-time jobs you can get depend on your Japanese language ability. As a native English speaker you can also teach ESL classes on the side. This would be a great way to get some experience if you plan to eventually look for full-time work as a teacher.

There's an overwhelming number of language schools out there and considering how most people have only attended just one, it's hard to find accurate comparisons. In Tokyo, some of the more popular schools are the Naganuma School, ISI Language School and Kai Language School. Choosing the best school for you is something you'll have to decide based on where you want to live and what your learning goals are. If you want to use a language school mainly for the visa and a chance to live in Japan, the price should be the main thing to keep an eye on.

Keep in mind, however, that once you get a student visa, you'll be expected to be a dedicated full-time student and your school will likely take attendance very seriously.

Once you get accepted to the school of your choice, you'll need to begin the application process for your student visa. A student visa is required for anyone studying full-time in Japan for over 3 months. Take a look at the beginning of Chapter 8 for a general overview on how the process works. The school that's sponsoring you should also be able to help guide you through the visa application process.[1]

Working Holiday

If you can't or don't want to be a student yet also want to avoid dealing with the stress of getting a normal working visa, consider coming to Japan as part of the Working Holiday program. Citizens of Australia, New Zealand, Canada, South Korea, France, Germany, the U.K., Ireland, Denmark and Taiwan are all eligible to come to Japan through the program. The U.S. is not part of this system, unfortunately, so U.S. citizens need to obtain a visa the old fashioned way. Be aware that there's a maximum age limit of 30 for applying, except for citizens of Ireland who must be 25 or younger.[2]

The whole purpose of the Working Holiday program is, as the name suggests, to work a little bit and have time and money left over to explore the country. Lots of people get jobs at places like ski resorts or hotels while traveling around Japan in their off time. The program was not designed to set you up working full-time for a major company, yet there are interestingly no restrictions on how long you can work. Therefore, it's not uncommon for people on Working Holiday visas to get full-time teaching jobs. There are also virtually no limitations on the jobs you're allowed to get with the visa but working at bars or hostess clubs is generally prohibited. That doesn't stop people from doing it anyway, however.

A university degree is not required to get a Working Holiday Visa which means that coming through this program is one of the few ways you can legally teach here without a bachelors degree. But be aware that when your visa runs out it probably won't be possible to switch over to a normal Specialist in Humanities Visa without a degree. If you really want to stay in Japan long-term then you should work on getting that degree first.

Getting the Working Holiday Visa itself is usually a piece of cake but people in the program still have to find a job just like everyone else. It's therefore vital that you bring over enough funds with you to survive for awhile. The following chapters discuss how to hunt for teaching jobs, how much money you should bring and how to find a place to live. Later on you'll find info on alternatives to teaching if you want to give something like graphic design or IT work a go.

2

HUNTING FOR TEACHING JOBS

As will be reiterated many times throughout this book, coming to Japan as an English teacher is the easiest way to obtain your first working visa. Even if teaching isn't your passion, many people simply use it as a jumping-off point for entering their desired industry further down the road.

But just how should one go about finding a teaching job? And what's all this stuff about, ALT, JET and eikaiwa? What's the difference and how much do they pay? Can a job be found online or is it necessary to visit Japan? I'll be answering all of those questions and a lot more in the next couple of chapters.

Getting a Teaching Certificate

If you don't have any experience teaching English and are coming to Japan for the first time, I highly recommend obtaining some kind of English teaching certificate before applying for jobs. To be clear, the Japanese government does not require you to have a certificate before granting you a visa. In many Asian countries and in other parts of the world, you absolutely need to be certified before you're allowed to teach English legally. While it's not mandatory here, being a certified ESL teacher will help you stand out from the other applicants and also prepare you for the job itself.

Employers taking an interest in certification is only a recent trend in Japan. Up until several years ago, whether or not a teacher was certified made no difference to most ESL companies and many employers had never even heard of a CELTA. If you find some info online from a decade ago about working in Japan, you may read that becoming certified is a waste of time. That may have been true at one point but things are different now. As the competition for ESL jobs becomes increasingly fierce, certified teachers are gradually becoming the standard in the Japanese ESL industry. Especially if you lack prior Japan experience, being certified shows your prospective employer that you're serious about the job.

But which certificate should you go for? TESL, TEFL, TESOL or CELTA? Doing a quick online search, the sheer amount of different programs being offered around the world is overwhelming. It's also not always clear which ones are actually going to be recognized and accepted by your employer. Generally, TESL, TEFL and TESOL all mean pretty much the same thing, and simply refer to any certificate to teach English as a second or foreign language. CELTA is a very specific type of teaching certificate which is accredited by Cambridge University. Due to its affiliation with Cambridge, CELTA is regarded by many as the most prestigious.

The CELTA Course

CELTA is the certificate I ended up aiming for myself. With the CELTA program you have the option of taking an intensive one month course or spreading it out over a few months. I decided to go with the one month course and I can honestly say it was one of the most intense and exhausting months of my life. You'll be spending nearly every single waking moment on getting that certificate and you'll hardly get the chance to interact with anyone outside of the course. At least you'll likely become close with the other participants. I was lucky enough to be in a group with some great people, some of whom I still keep in touch with today.

The CELTA course involves several demo lessons amounting to a total of 6 teaching hours over the month. You'll be teaching a group of about 20 or so adult students with your peers and instructor also present. During your lessons, the other participants will be taking notes on your strong and weak points to discuss with you after the class. If you've never taught in front of large groups before it can be extremely nerve-racking. But sometimes you'll simply be too sleepy to feel nervous, as there will be a ton of homework to complete the night before.

Before each of your lessons you'll be required to write pages and pages of details on specific grammar points or vocabulary that you plan to teach. This, along with a detailed lesson plan, must be submitted to your instructor that morning. There are also a number of weekend assignments that can be incredibly time consuming. The course was so intense that when I try to look back on specific details it's all just kind of a blur. But in the end I did manage to pass, and only one person out of my group of 20 or so participants dropped out. If you're not able to put your entire life aside for one month then I suggest you go for one of the slower-paced courses.

Another well-known certificate is the Trinity TEFL, accredited by Trinity College London. The Trinity TEFL is very similar to the CELTA in regards to course length, teaching hours and other general requirements needed to pass. Trinity TEFL is just about as well-known internationally as the CELTA so I'd recommend going for either one depending on whichever's more convenient for you. There are plenty of other TEFL or TESOL courses you'll come across during your research but it's best to make sure your certificate is accredited and will actually be recognized by employers abroad. Beware of budget online courses that will grant you a certificate nobody's ever heard of. There are, however, some online courses accredited by well-known organizations or universities, although they might not always include hands-on teaching experience.

Where to Look for Teaching Jobs Online

Gaijinpot (gaijinpot.com)

This is the most popular site for job hunting in Japan. There's an abundance of ESL job postings and you can also find IT, recruiting and other random positions.

Before applying you'll need to upload your resume to the site using Gaijinpot's own format. This makes it very easy to apply quickly and easily for any position that catches your eye, but the downside is that everyone else is doing the same thing. Most decent-looking positions get flooded with dozens or even hundreds of applications. That doesn't necessarily mean that you don't stand a chance, though. I've been called into interviews before for some positions that had a couple hundred other applicants, so don't lose hope.

Another unique feature of Gaijinpot is that you can make your resume public. In some cases a company may actually be the one to find you!

O-Hayo Sensei (ohayosensei.com)

This is an online magazine that sends info about open teaching positions to your inbox. You can also view the latest issue online. There are postings for work all over the country, even in rural areas. Naturally, most job postings will be for the more populated areas like Kanto or Kansai.

Craigslist (tokyo.craigslist.jp, osaka.craigslist.jp, etc.)

A lot of companies don't bother posting on Craigslist but it wouldn't hurt to check for updates daily. Be aware of anonymous postings in which a company deliberately leaves out their name. From personal experience, whenever I contacted one of these mystery companies they almost always turned out to be one of the especially shady ones. Obviously, they don't want to be Googled right away so they keep their name private in the job ad. Go ahead and write them if you feel like it, but be sure to do your research once you find out who they really are.

Dave's ESL Cafe (www.eslcafe.com)

This is an international site for ESL teachers all over the world. It lacks a dedicated section for teaching positions in Japan. You'll have to go to the "International Job Board" and then scroll through all of the listings to find the ones relevant to you.

They do have a section of their forums dedicated to Japan which I recommend checking out. You can find some useful tips on teaching as well as information about certain companies you should either apply to or avoid.

Japan English Teacher (japanenglishteacher.com)

This a clear, easy-to-use site but there just aren't that many positions listed at any given time.

TokyoFREEads (tokyofreeads.com/teaching-jobs)

There are a lot of positions posted on here but there's strangely no indication of when each posting was uploaded. There's no way of telling if that sweet position you've just come across was posted today or sometime last year.

Kansai FREEads (kansaifreeads.com/teaching-jobs)

This is just the Kansai version of TokyoFREEads.

Kansai Flea Market (www.kfm.red/)

There are a lot of job postings here for all over the Kansai region. This should be one of your main go-to sites if you're living in or are open to working in Kansai.

KansaiScene (kansaiscene.com)

Another Kansai-based site. There are several positions posted here but not nearly as many as on sites like Gaijinpot.

Daijob (www.daijob.com)

This is a well-known job-hunting site but it's more intended for highly-skilled professionals, bilingual people or those that already have years of experience in Japan. There are occasionally teaching jobs posted so it wouldn't hurt to check periodically.

Metropolis Classifieds (classifieds.metropolis.co.jp)

There are hardly enough jobs posted here at all for it to warrant a mention, but since it's free to look at you might as well bookmark it. The main web site/magazine is a good resource for learning about Japanese culture or local events.

Applying From Abroad

For a number of reasons, I recommend coming to Japan as a tourist to look for work. The main reason is that coming here in person shows that you're really serious about finding employment in Japan. Second of all, there are already so many resident foreigners here job hunting already. It can be very hard to compete with these other applicants while you're still back in your home country.

That being said, coming to Japan as a tourist and attempting to find work within 90 days can be risky. If you're not yet willing to take that risk then there are a number of companies that organize recruitment drives throughout North America, Australia, the UK and other parts of Europe. If one or more of these companies are coming to your town then it would be a good idea to meet with them for an interview or at least to get some more information.

Below is a list of companies that send recruiters abroad. Even if you're not able to meet with them in your town, many of the major companies also accept online applications from those not yet in Japan.

AEON

- Major eikaiwa chain
- Schedule periodic recruitment drives

throughout the USA, UK, Canada and Australia
- Accept online applications

ALTIA

- ALT dispatch company that mostly focuses on the Chubu and Kansai regions
- Have recruiters that visit cities in the US such as Chicago, Charlotte and LA
- They also sometimes send people to London

ECC

- Major eikaiwa chain
- Have recruiting drives in Canada (Toronto and Vancouver) and the USA (NYC and LA)

Gaba

- Another big eikaiwa chain
- Organize information seminars where you can meet a recruiter in the UK and Australia

Interac

- The biggest ALT dispatch company

- Visit countries like the USA, Canada, UK, Ireland, Spain and Czech Republic
- People in the Philippines can apply through a third party recruiter called Chesham

JET

- This is the government-sponsored ALT program (There is an entire section on the JET Program in Chapter 4, so have a look there for more information)

Westgate

- This is a company that sets up teachers with university teaching positions
- A master's degree and years of experience are often required (refer to Chapter 4 for more info)

When hunting for jobs online, you may also come across some small schools in rural areas that accept applicants from abroad. This could be because of the small number of foreigners living in those areas. However, whether you're applying from abroad to a small rural school or a huge company, always be a bit cautious and do the proper research in advance.

Why would an employer go through the trouble of recruiting people from abroad and handling all the paperwork for their visas? There are so many experienced teachers here with valid working visas already, so why would this be worth all the effort?

Here are a couple of possible explanations:

a) That company has a dubious reputation amongst teachers in Japan so they recruit abroad where not many people have heard of them.

b) The more they help the teacher from abroad get set up here with a job and an apartment, the more reliant that teacher becomes on them. If the company then decides to not follow through with some of the things they've promised, like certain benefits or even paying the agreed-upon salary, the teacher has little recourse to take action or switch jobs.

c) Experienced long-term residents already have local connections, some knowledge of the language and a basic understanding of Japanese labor laws. As a result, a lot of these sleazier companies prefer to snatch up vulnerable newcomers instead.

I'm not saying this is the case for all companies that actively recruit or accept applications from abroad. In any case, please do your research on the company before you apply and especially before you sign a contract. Check Glassdoor, blogs and TEFL forums to see what people have been saying about whichever company you apply to.

Job Hunting as a Tourist

This is the best way to find a job here but it also comes with a number of risks. First of all, most people are not allowed to spend more than 90 days here as a tourist. Therefore, timing is everything. Don't make the mistake of just showing up in Japan to look for work as soon as you're able to. It's important to make the most of your time by flying over just before peak hiring season.

In Japan, April 1st is the beginning of the country's fiscal year. New recruits hired by companies generally start working on this date and it's also when the school year begins. Therefore, the best time to come for work, assuming you can only stay here for 90 days, is in late January or early February.

Besides April, September is the most common period for starting new jobs and some ALT positions also begin around this time. If you can't make it in the beginning of the year, you might want to visit sometime in the summer to hopefully schedule some interviews for jobs starting in September.

Eikaiwa jobs tend to hire all year round and so do some jobs in other industries. I've started new jobs before in both May and June (not of the same year). This was after already having experience and a valid visa, however, which made those job hunts much easier than when I first came as a tourist.

For citizens of certain countries, it may be possible to apply for an additional 90 day extension as a tourist without needing to leave Japan. This applies to citizens of the UK, Ireland, Germany, Switzerland, Austria, Lichtenstein and Mexico. Having 180 days to job hunt gives you much more freedom and flexibility than the average person. But considering how expensive Japan is, you definitely don't want to find yourself without an income for 6 months!

It's important to note that while working on a tourist visa is illegal, looking for work and interviewing for jobs on a tourist visa is perfectly legal. However, to avoid any complications at the airport, I recommend that you DO NOT mention your job hunt to the airport immigration officers. They may just wrongly assume that you intend to work illegally. Whenever they ask, tell them that you're just in the country for tourism.

<u>Another important point</u>: You're technically required to have an onward ticket to another country scheduled for sometime before your tourist visa runs out. I've never been asked to provide this by immigration whenever I've entered Japan as a tourist. However, every time I fly to Japan from another country I get asked to show proof of an onward ticket or a valid visa before I can get my boarding pass. I recommend you buy a refundable onward ticket to be on the safe side. As soon as you arrive in Japan, cancel your ticket and get the full refund.

As for where to live during your job hunt, check out Chapter 5 for info on share houses and other short-term accommodation.

"How Much Money Should I Bring?"

If you're coming to look for work as a tourist, I recommend bringing a minimum of ¥500,000 for Tokyo and at least ¥400,000 for cheaper cities like Osaka or Nagoya. That's **not** including the plane tickets. And those amounts should be considered the bare minimum needed to scrape by. Definitely come with more if you can.

At the time of writing the yen is still pretty weak. If it stays this way for awhile then converting your savings from dollars, euros or pounds should work out well in your favor. On the other hand, prices in Japan have also been rising due to inflation and sales tax increases. The sales tax was recently increased from 5% to 8% and from 2017 it's scheduled to rise again to 10%. During the recent tax increase, many stores took the opportunity to also raise their base prices, thinking that the average consumer wouldn't notice. I expect something similar to happen again in 2017.

In the Kanto area, Tokyo is obviously going to be the most expensive city but a lot of people base themselves in neighboring prefectures like Chiba or Saitama. You can save a lot on rent and groceries by living in suburban or rural places, but transport to Tokyo or wherever your interview might be can become costly. If you choose Kansai for your job search and live in central Osaka or Kyoto, you can easily get around those cities by bicycle. You may not want to do that to get to an interview on a hot day in your best suit, but it's still a possibility.

Here's a basic breakdown of how much daily life could cost you, even on a relatively frugal lifestyle. I'm going to use central Tokyo as an example. A guest house/share house that's in the central 23 wards could cost you ¥40,000 - ¥50,000 a month, plus a few *man* (1 *man* = 10,000) yen deposit. Food in Japan can get expensive, especially if you want to eat nutritious things like fruits and vegetables. Eating mostly pasta, rice and instant noodles will save you a ton of money, but let's assume you want to eat relatively healthy. And let's also include drinks in this total figure. If you keep your food and drink budget at around ¥2,000 total per day, that's around ¥180,000 spent on food over three months.

Transport around the city adds up to a lot, and if you're going all over town for interviews, expect to pay from around ¥400 - ¥1000 a day on transport. Some days will cost more and some less. If you can buy or rent a bicycle or don't mind walking long distances, you could save a bit of money every day. Tokyo is massive, however, so biking everywhere isn't always reasonable.

Rent, food and transport are just the basic essentials but already add up to a little under ¥400,000 for the 90 days you have for your job hunt! If you do accomplish your goal of finding a job, it's likely that you won't even receive your first paycheck until the middle or end of the following month.

It's wise to be frugal during this period, but if it's your first time in Japan you should also have enough extra cash to go out and see the city. Museums can cost you one or two thousand yen, while temples and shrines are generally free. You're also going to want to go out drinking and experience some of the nightlife, if that's your thing. Set aside extra money especially for this in advance because a basic night out in Tokyo or Osaka can be surprisingly expensive. Even a beer at a basic bar or club can cost around ¥500 - ¥700, with cocktails costing slightly more. If you go to a club with live DJ's, don't be surprised to have to pay between ¥2,000 - ¥4,000 at the door. After paying for cover, drinks and transport, it's not uncommon to spend up to ¥10,000 on a single Saturday night!

Live concerts can cost even more than clubs but you probably won't be spending as much on alcohol. Famous international bands can demand prices of ¥8,000 - ¥10,000 per ticket. Karaoke nights are cheaper than live music events but it all depends on how much you order to drink. Before going out, I recommend putting the maximum amount of cash you're willing to spend that night in your wallet or purse and promise yourself not to visit an ATM. If you're the type that doesn't drink or like to go out, you're going to do pretty well with money here.

Choosing Where to Live

Japan is a fairly large country, but Kansai and Kanto are the two most well-known regions and have also been historic cultural rivals. As someone who's lived in both, I'll provide a quick list of pros and cons for those still trying to decide:

Kansai

Pros:
- Friendly people, possibly the warmest and most open in the country
- Cheaper rent than Tokyo
- Access to rich cultural heritage sites in Kyoto and Nara
- Contains 3 major cities (Osaka, Kyoto and Kobe) which are all very distinct from one another yet easily accessible by train
- Even if you live in central Osaka, you can get to the mountains in about 30 minutes by train
- Delicious food

Cons:
- Simply not as many job opportunities as in Kanto
- The cities can start to feel too small after awhile
- A lot of urban areas, especially in Osaka, are pretty run-down by Japanese standards
- Statistically, Osaka has Japan's highest crime rate, although you're unlikely to encounter much worse than bicycle theft

Kanto

Pros:
- The Tokyo region offers the most job opportunities in Japan by far
- If you like nightlife, music and entertainment, many international artists stop by Tokyo that don't always visit other Japanese cities
- Amazingly efficient transport system
- Contains more greenery and parks than Osaka

Cons:
- Has the highest rent and livings costs in Japan, with only slightly higher salaries
- Difficult to access the beach or mountains, especially from central Tokyo
- Insanely crowded
- Many people have surprisingly bad manners, especially on the roads, in the street and in train stations
- Generally colder people than in Kansai and your neighbors may even ignore your greetings
- Lots of superficial, materialistic types
- Highly competitive

Clearly, Kansai is the winner here, at least in my opinion. While I do prefer Kansai overall, it just doesn't have all the opportunities that Tokyo has to offer, especially if you eventually decide to transition out of teaching.

Other options to consider:

Nagoya is an up-and-coming city that has even overtaken Osaka in terms of population. Personally, I find Nagoya to be a bit bland, with no real apparent local culture to speak of.

Sapporo is a really fun city with people just as friendly as in Osaka. It can get very, very cold up there, however, which can be a major turn-off for some people.

Okinawa is one of my favorite places in Japan and if you like tropical weather and beautiful beaches then you might want to give it a shot. With that said, it's also the poorest prefecture with the lowest wages.

Failing to Find a Job Within 90 Days

As I mentioned, most nationalities only have 90 days to stay in Japan as a tourist. While I still feel coming here in person is the best approach, three months is just not that much time to arrive in a new country, find a place to stay, send out resumes, go to interviews and apply for a visa. Consider getting a head start by mailing out your resumes shortly before your flight and letting the companies know exactly when you plan to arrive.

A lot of people don't find anything by the time their landing permit or tourist visa runs out. Unlike some other countries, you don't have to stay out of the country for another 90 days but can reset your landing permit as soon as you leave and come back. One option is to take a quick trip to the nearest country, South Korea, and then fly back to Japan a few days later. You can buy a round-trip ticket for ¥20,000 or so. However, I don't advise doing this more than once.

Immigration is well aware that some people are working illegally on tourist visas by making visa runs every few months. Even if you're just legally searching for jobs, making visa runs are much more difficult now. They probably won't say anything if you've just done it once, but they'll likely ask you a lot of questions the second time. If questioned, tell them that you love Japan and want to do some more traveling before going home. Or say that you're back for your friend's wedding. If things don't work out for you this time, you may want to try working in another Asian country and then come back to Japan after gaining some teaching experience.

Note: "Landing permit" and "tourist visa" are often used interchangeably. The landing permit is not technically a visa, just the stamp in your passport that allows you to stay for up to 90 days. If you're from a native English-speaking country or the EU, you likely won't need to apply for any visa to travel to Japan. You simply get a landing permit when you arrive, but many people refer to this as a "tourist visa" anyway.

3

THE APPLICATION AND INTERVIEW PROCESS

Writing Your Resume and Cover Letter

In Japan, a traditional resume is known as a *rirekisho*, but you won't need to make one of these when applying for English teaching positions. Even an English-language resume or CV, however, will require you to include more personal information than you might be used to or comfortable with. First of all, you'll need a picture of yourself (in business attire, of course) at the top of your resume. You'll also need to provide your age and marital status. Japanese people even include their blood type but as a foreigner you won't be expected to go quite that far.

As you would back home, be sure to include a cover letter along with your resume. I usually include the cover letter in the text of my email with my resume as a .pdf file attachment. On sites like Gaijinpot, there's a special section where you can paste your cover letter and even save various templates.

The key to writing a good cover letter is explaining how you're the right person for the position without resorting to bragging, which is especially looked down upon in Japanese culture. In the very first sentence you want to mention your name and TEFL certifications, and then write something like:

"I would like to express my interest in your available position. I feel that I can make a positive contribution to [company name] by..."

You then want to briefly summarize your skills and background. In the next paragraph you might want to talk about your experience in or with Japan or bring up relevant travel experience to demonstrate that you can handle living outside your comfort zone. Also add how this experience would help you in the classroom. Near the end, include your contact information and how and when you can be reached. Finally, thank them in advance for taking the time to look at your attached resume.

In Japan it doesn't matter much if your resume is 2 or even 3 pages long, so don't worry about trying to keep everything on a single page. Just as in your cover letter, be sure to include any prior teaching experience you may have, no matter how little. Include info on your teaching certification(s) and on any prior international or volunteer experience. Aside from how well you can teach, companies need to know you won't freak out in a new culture and environment and that you won't suddenly disappear after a few months.

If you're applying for both eikaiwa and ALT positions, which you should be, make a resume and cover letter template for each. Remember that eikaiwa schools have students of all ages taking one-on-one lessons or in smaller groups. ALT jobs consist of teaching large groups of young learners in a traditional school setting. In contrast, most TEFL certificate courses focus on teaching groups of adults. If you're a certified teacher applying for an eikaiwa job, talk about how you already have prior experience teaching adults. When applying for an ALT position, you can instead put the emphasis on how you're capable of managing larger classrooms.

Resume Sample Template

Please refrain from copying this exact template and my exact words. Feel free to use it as a reference, but at least change it up enough to make it your own.

Your Name *(Put your picture somewhere here)*
123456 Your Address
Your.email.address@gmail.com
090-555-6543

Personal Details
(A lot of this information would never be included on
your resume back home, but this is all standard info in Japan)

Nationality:
Place of Birth:
Passport Expiration:
Date of Birth:
Age:
Marital Status:

Visa Status:

Objective:
Highly motivated EFL teacher with experience tutoring children and adults seeks to utilize and improve skills at a lan guage school in Japan

Education

TEFL Certificate Program: Bangkok, Thailand
University of Cambridge Certificate in English Language Teaching to Adults, PASS: July, 2016

d) Learned a variety of teaching methods, classroom management and lesson-planning skills
e) Taught groups of pre-intermediate and upper-intermediate level students for a total of 6 hours of observed and assessed teaching practice

Watashino University
Bachelor of Arts in Japanese Literature: June, 2016

Work and Volunteer Experience

(If this is going to be your first job after university, put an em phasis on any previous volunteer or international experience that you've had. If you've done anything related to teaching or tutoring, emphasize that as well)

Volunteer Teacher (Houston, Texas): Jan. - Aug. 2015
Volunteer ESL Teacher at Local Community Center

- Designed and carried out comprehensive lesson plans to teach various grammar and vocabulary points to learners of all ages
- Helped young learners and adults improve their English speaking and reading abilities through conversation practice, texts and games

University Internship (Toronto, Canada): Spring 2015
Intern at local newspaper

- (*Emphasize not just what you did, but what it is that you accomplished*)
-

International Volunteer (Kaigai, Gaikoku): Autumn 2014
Volunteer

- Volunteered on a remote island to give English lessons and help build schools for impoverished members of a local tribe
- Designed a comprehensive action plan for ways future projects could further benefit the community

Skills and Experience

- Japanese ability: Passed JLPT(?), able to function with Japanese staff
- Experience teaching English to children and adults of various nationalities
- Proficient in Microsoft Office and Adobe Photoshop

Hobbies and Interests

- Photography
- Travel
- Music
- Anime (*if this is your hobby, maybe put this last*)

References available upon request

The Interview

Japan is a very formal country so it should go without saying that you need to put on your best business attire for the interview. You should already have this packed in your suitcase before you arrive, but there are many, many suit stores in Japan should you need to do some shopping after getting here.

If you're a man, you might want to shave off your beard just in case. I've seen plenty of teachers with facial hair, however, so if you're intent on keeping it, just make sure it's very neat and trimmed. For ladies, avoid putting on too much makeup or perfume for the interview.

It's best to print out a couple of copies of your resume in advance - one for you and another for the interviewer(s). You can put your resume on an SD card or USB drive and print them out at any 7-11 if you don't have a printer at home (make sure they're .pdf format). Do this in advance and don't let this make you late!

Punctuality is extremely important in Japan and even showing up at the scheduled time is considered 'late.' Being on time in Japan really means showing up 10 - 15 minutes early. It might be a good idea to walk by the interview location the day before so you know exactly how to get there and how long the commute is going to take. I've been late to an interview once thanks to the Google Maps GPS sending me in the opposite direction, so don't rely too much on your phone either.

Some interviews will require that you do a demo lesson. In some cases you'll be asked to prepare something in advance while other times you'll be shown the material for the very first time at the interview. Either way, the company should let you know about this ahead of time, although I can recall having been put on the spot a few times before.

Even without a demo lesson, you may be asked to take a short quiz to prove that you know the fundamentals of English grammar. If you've taken a TEFL or CELTA course and it's still fresh in your mind, what you've learned there will come in handy. If you're not certified and have never taught before, I recommend going over some TEFL or English grammar books before your interviews. You may not have to do a demo lesson or even take a quiz but the interviewer could potentially ask you to explain how you'd teach a particular grammar point or elicit vocabulary from your students.

If you have prior Japan experience or wrote somewhere on your resume that you've studied Japanese, don't be surprised if you get asked some questions in Japanese during the interview. Most English teaching jobs do not officially require Japanese and many eikaiwa schools ban the use of it during their lessons, but many companies secretly do appreciate teachers with Japanese ability. It demonstrates dedication to staying in the country and sensitivity to the culture. If you become an ALT, most of your coworkers will not speak any English so teachers with Japanese ability are highly valued.

Some interviews have a couple of different stages requiring you to come back 2 or 3 times. Depending on the interview, it could be one-on-one, two-on-one, or you might be interviewing with several other teachers at the same time. I recommend taking a look at the Japan section of sites like Dave's ESL Café where you can find first-hand accounts of people's interview experiences with certain companies.

Here are some questions you should prepare yourself for:

- *Why did you leave your last job?* (If applicable)
- *What are your hobbies?*
- *Why do you want to teach English?*
- *Do you see yourself teaching long term?*
- *What would you say if* x *and* y *are asked of you, even if they're not mentioned in your contract?*

Be sure to memorize every little detail about your resume, as you'll surely be asked some very specific questions about it as well!

I understand that many of you are not especially passionate about teaching and will be applying for positions mainly for the visa and to pay the bills. I was the same and a majority of people teaching English in Japan probably are too. The people interviewing you are also well aware that teaching is not exactly everyone's dream job. If asked, I recommend you tell them that you really do want to be a teacher and plan on sticking to teaching for a few years at least. Why would they bother to hire you if you said otherwise? Also, have responses planned in advance in case they ask you what your favorite thing about teaching is. To avoid appearing too insincere, try to redirect the conversation back to your enthusiasm for living and working in Japan and away from teaching itself.

If you're a hardcore anime otaku, I would choose not to reveal this. Anime is part of Japan's mainstream culture but anime otaku are generally looked down upon here. You also don't want the interviewers to think you're in the country only for that reason. It's fine to go ahead and mention anime as one of your hobbies, but be sure to talk about your other interests and some of the other things you like about Japan. Your passion for anime could work in your favor if you're talented at drawing anime characters, for example. You could explain how your artistic ability would help you relate to younger students and get them excited for your lessons.

As mentioned already, it's also extremely important that you demonstrate flexibility, especially in regards to location. If you insist on only taking a position in the central part of a big city, the company will see you as inflexible and not as a team player. Sure, tell them your preference but also emphasize that you're open to anywhere. The same applies to your work schedule as well. Most eikaiwa companies will expect you to work Saturdays and sometimes even on Sundays. Hopefully you'll get a couple of job offers so you can choose the position that works best for you.

Good luck! がんばれ!

4

TEACHING JOB OVERVIEW

The two most common job opportunities for newcomers to Japan are becoming an eikaiwa teacher or an Assistant Language Teacher (ALT). An ALT teaches at a Japanese elementary, junior high or high school while an eikaiwa teacher works at a private English conversation school. This chapter focuses on the differences between the two and the general work environment you can expect from each. I also go over some other types of teaching opportunities in the final section.

Teaching English Conversation (Eikaiwa)

Being an eikaiwa, or English conversation teacher generally means working at a private conversation school run by a company. There are some schools exclusively for children and some exclusively for adults, but many of the major chains take on students of all ages. It's not uncommon to be doing the hokey pokey with a group of 5 year olds one moment and then be discussing cross-cultural business etiquette with your adult student the next.

Eikaiwa schools have their own schedule and national holidays and weekends don't apply, with the exception of New Years. You'll most likely be working every Saturday with Sunday and Monday as your days off. While the weekdays will have you coming in at around noon or 1pm and working until late, you'll likely need to come in at around 9am on Saturdays. If you're not naturally a morning person, waking up extra early on this one day a week can be a difficult adjustment. Saturdays are also usually the busiest days, so don't count on meeting up with your friends on Friday nights anymore.

When working at eikaiwa jobs you'll typically be working directly for the company that employs you, although dispatch companies hiring eikaiwa teachers do exist. In contrast to being an ALT, you'll have other foreign teachers to interact with on the job but your lunch breaks will usually be at different times.

In general, eikaiwa teachers teach more hours per week than ALT's. Some days can be so busy that you just simply won't have time to prepare for every lesson. This is especially difficult at the beginning of the job as you're still familiarizing yourself with the text books and also the strengths and weaknesses of each student. Once you get the hang of things and have already taught certain grammar points several times before, improvising will come as second nature.

Eikaiwa work consists of many one-on-one lessons but there are a fair amount of group lessons too. You might teach a larger group of up to 7 or 8 adults in the afternoon but then just teach classes of 1 - 3 students for the rest of the day. Or, you may get stuck teaching groups of several children. These can either be fun, exhausting or both, depending on the circumstances. You always need to keep your eye on all the students as the classrooms are often tiny and were never designed for a bunch of kids to be running around in. I once had a student trip and smack his head right into the wall during a group activity. I then had to explain to the rest of my students that day why the carpet was stained with blood!

Eikaiwa is one of your only options if you want to work in a big city. Another positive of the job is that you might get to meet some interesting adult students and have more insightful conversations with your students than you ever could as an ALT.

Becoming an ALT

Being an ALT means teaching in a typical Japanese school, usually public but sometimes private. Certain companies or Boards of Education (BoE's) use other acronyms like NET (Native English Teacher) or AET (Assistant English Teacher) but they all refer to the same job. Teachers that are part of the JET program are also ALT's but are commonly just referred to as "JET's". Nowadays, most of the ALT's in Japan are employed by dispatch companies.

ALT dispatch companies have contracts with local city or prefectural BoE's and handle all of the hiring and training of native teachers. Dispatch companies get paid a hefty sum by the local BoE and then pay a smaller portion of that to the teachers as their monthly salary. When working for a dispatch company it's important to remember that you are basically your employer's product. Your employer's customer, the school and BoE, is going to have certain expectations for this product that they're paying good money for. They often won't know or care what your actual salary is and it's not something you're supposed to talk about with anyone at your school.

School Structure

At Japanese schools, students are divided into classes, or *kumi* and study with the same group of classmates in the same room for the entire year. This system applies from elementary school all the way up through high school. Students stay in the same place except for special classes like PE. As an ALT, you will always be moving from classroom to classroom according to the day's schedule.

The key word in Assistant Language Teacher is *assistant*. ALT's at public schools aren't allowed to teach on their own and must always teach classes together with the Japanese Teacher of English, or JTE. Therefore, your main job isn't necessarily to teach English *per se*, but to do whatever the JTE tells you to do. The JTE may ask for your input and collaborate with you on planning and carrying out the lesson, or they may do almost all of the planning and teaching themselves. Hardly being expected to do anything at all other than read vocabulary lists aloud to the class is commonly referred to in the industry as being a "human tape recorder." The main challenge of these lessons is keeping yourself from falling asleep while standing.

On the other end of the spectrum, the JTE might ask you to both plan and execute the entire lesson while they chill out in the corner. Regardless of what's requested of you, your workload is not going to effect your salary at all.

Also understand that you'll likely be the only foreigner at your school and may even be the only teacher in your age range. As a result, ALT work can be pretty lonely on a day-to-day basis. It's best to keep yourself busy by working on something productive during your free time.

The best part of being an ALT over an eikaiwa teacher is that you get weekends and national holidays off. There are also long winter and summer breaks. Depending on your employer, however, you may or may not get paid for these vacation periods.

Remember, there are an enormous amount of variables with ALT jobs. Even two teachers employed by the same company, working in the same town and making the same salary could have completely different experiences.

The JET Program

The Japan Exchange and Teaching Program, or JET, is probably the most prestigious and sought-after teaching program in the country. Why? The program pays more than most ALT jobs and it's sponsored by the Japanese government, which sees the program as more of a cultural exchange rather than purely as a business. As a result, the JET program has a much better reputation than most dispatch and eikaiwa companies. JET is also one of the only programs that actually pays for their teachers' international plane tickets to come to Japan. They'll even set you up with an apartment and everything else you need to get started. Furthermore, JET teachers' salaries are untaxed.

The program accepts people from all over the world and not just from native English-speaking countries. It should go without saying that teachers must have at least near-native English ability to be accepted. On the topic of language ability, Japanese is not a requirement but definitely a plus. Having at least made an effort to study Japanese will demonstrate a genuine interest in the country and culture.

The main downside to JET would be having no say in where you live. If you absolutely need to live in a city like Tokyo, Osaka, or Nagoya at all costs then the JET program isn't for you. There's still a chance you could be placed in a city, however, and I've even met one JET that got set up with an apartment in central Shibuya. But it's far more likely you'll be in an area surrounded for miles and miles by rice paddies. Undoubtedly, living in the countryside can still be an enjoyable and enriching experience. But if you're very much a city person then you might want to think twice before applying.

Several thousands of applications are sent in to JET each year. The organization does not reveal the number of applicants that get accepted, only that it is "very competitive."[3] The application process is infamous for the loads of paperwork required. You need to submit all sorts of documents like a copy of your passport, educational transcripts, proof of your bachelor's degree, recommendation letters and even a form on which you must self-assess your own health.[4] If you're a US citizen you'll need to provide an FBI criminal background check. The process shouldn't be too difficult but it can take up to a couple of months so it's important to time everything right. For a detailed list on the documents required for your application, look at the official JET Program web site of your home country.

In addition to gathering documents and finishing all the paperwork, you also need to submit an essay called the "Statement of Purpose." In the essay, which can be no longer than 2 pages, you must demonstrate a genuine interest in Japanese culture. You're supposed to talk about what sparked your interest in Japan and what intrigues you most about it. Giving simple answers like 'video games' or 'manga' is probably not what they're looking for. You're also expected to provide examples of relevant skills and experiences that show you can both handle teaching a classroom full of students and also daily life in a foreign culture. And don't forget to include the ways in which you hope to impact your local community in Japan and also what you expect to get out of the program personally.[5]

If you're one of the lucky few to get invited to an interview, you'll have to make your way to the nearest Japanese consulate or embassy on your own dime. At the interview there will likely be three people asking you questions. Like with any job interview, make sure you know the information on your own application form like the back of your hand. If you're asked about it, you need to be able to mention any specific details on the spot. You should do your best to demonstrate interest in Japan and show how flexible and adaptable you are in regards to location and living away from your family or partner.

One common criticism of JET is that the program is more or less designed to advertise Japan and Japanese culture to the JET's themselves. Teachers come, get slightly overpaid for easy work, experience a bit of the culture and then return home after a couple of years, raving to their friends and family about how awesome Japan is. JET has always been more of a promotional tool than an actual teaching business. As a result, many JET's are somewhat sheltered from the reality of typical Japanese work culture. Former JET's may be in for quite a shock when eventually moving onto eikaiwa work or becoming a regular salaryman at a Japanese company.

Other Kinds of Teaching Jobs

Eikaiwa, dispatch ALT and JET aren't the only options out there. Below is a list of some other teaching jobs you may want to consider. Be aware that not all of these are necessarily better than eikaiwa or ALT work in regards to salary or working environment. As always, do a lot of your own research before applying to or accepting any new position.

Preschool/Kindergarten Teacher

There are quite a few opportunities available for teaching very young learners. Some preschools and kindergartens operate exclusively in English and require native

English-speaking or bilingual staff. There are also preschools tied to bigger international schools that may be looking for foreign teachers. Depending on the preschool, you may be teaching all Japanese children or mostly foreign children growing up here. Salaries are usually around the standard rate, but there is one well-known company called JICE which pays teachers around ¥290,000 per month.

It should go without saying, but only consider these positions if you really love constantly being around large groups of young children. Admittedly, I don't fit into this category but I did go to an interview once at a preschool back when I was very desperate for a visa. I thought it would be a typical job interview but they actually had me spend the entire day there so that I fully understood just what I might be getting myself into. The kids were great but I barely lasted a day even as an observer. To sum it up: lots of singing, dancing, watching Wiggles videos and even diaper changing! It seemed like much more work, not to mention messier and smellier, than a typical eikaiwa gig for the same pay. But if you really love kids then go for it.

Business English

Teaching business English usually involves teaching groups of salarymen at their company headquarters, or sometimes smaller groups and individual lessons at a local coffee shop. The hourly pay is generally much better than other types of teaching, with teachers earning from around ¥4,000 - ¥6,000 an hour. Actual business experience is generally preferred but most employers are aware of the fact that few English teachers have ever worked outside of the ESL industry. Prior eikaiwa experience plus a basic understanding of Japan and its business customs are often enough to qualify. If you've taught at an eikaiwa then you've probably already taught at least a couple of business lessons before, something you should mention during your interview.

The downside of teaching business English is that it's usually nothing more than a part-time or contract job. You may only be able to get a few regular lessons per week or get hired for a one-off intensive course that lasts a week or a month. Due to the unstable nature of the job, most teachers just do some extra business lessons on top of other full-time work.

Freelancing

This is a pretty broad category, but freelance teachers typically string together a combination of part-time jobs and private lessons. It's possible to earn more than a standard teaching salary this way. The downside is that if some of your students quit, you'll need to spend time and energy looking for replacements to replenish that lost income.

Freelance teachers often do a combination of business lessons, casual cafe lessons and maybe one or two full days at an eikaiwa school somewhere. When becoming a freelance teacher it's also worth it to familiarize yourself with popular ESL exams such as the TOEIC or Eiken, as specialized exam prep lessons are in high demand. If you don't want to put in all the effort to find private students yourself, there are even a number of companies that set you up with students for one-on-one lessons in casual settings. Some companies even have you going around to families' homes a couple times a week to teach their children.

If your total salary adds up to enough for the immigration authorities to be happy then you should be able to successfully self-sponsor your visa. This is not something you're going to be able to do immediately after arriving here, however. A sustainable freelance schedule will take time and effort to build up, but it could eventually allow for a much more flexible schedule with better pay. You also get to avoid dealing with some of the shady practices that many full-time employers in the industry are known for.

Direct Hire ALT

Not all ALT's are employed by JET or dispatch companies. Some ALT's get hired directly by the local Board of Education. Since there's no middle man taking a cut from the salary, the pay is significantly higher than other ALT work. But direct hire positions can be hard to come by and many people just come across direct hire positions by chance. Perhaps they've been working through a dispatch company at the same school for a number of years. If that BoE ends their relationship with the dispatch company, the teacher may be offered a job as a direct hire.

Some ALT's who move from dispatch to direct hire discover the job to be much more work than they bargained for. While the pay is higher, the ALT's will be expected to work longer hours than before, similar to those of a regular teacher in Japan. They may also be expected to show up on weekends and holidays to help organize extracurricular activities. On the plus side, the ALT will have more of a chance to become involved with the local community, potentially enriching their overall Japan experience.

University Teaching

If teaching is your passion and you want to be a teacher long term in Japan, consider aiming for a teaching position at a Japanese university. It's nearly impossible to get one of these jobs without at least an MA in TEFL/TESL, however. Ambitious eikaiwa teachers often take online MA courses outside of their full-time jobs. Some universities even require their professors to have at least a few publications in academic journals. Japanese language fluency may also be required.

Competition for full-time university teaching positions is notoriously fierce. In the beginning, some people may have to string together part-time jobs at different universities until they're experienced enough to be accepted somewhere full-time. If you know anybody currently teaching at university, they may be able to give you some leads on job openings before a position gets posted publicly.

One of the companies you'll likely come across when searching for a university teaching position is Westgate. Westgate is one of the few companies that hires from abroad and also reimburses international airfare. However, they only offer contracts per semester, so those looking for something stable and relatively long term may want to look elsewhere. On the other hand, if you're new to the country then it could be a good way to try out working in Japan for a few months before deciding if you want to stay longer.

Westgate instructors are also generally required to live in housing provided by the company, as this is another one of the ways the company makes a profit. The standard salary, at around ¥270,000 a month, is only slightly higher than that of ALT or eikaiwa work. This is much lower pay than a normal full-time university position but it's also an easier job to get.

A company like Westgate can be one way to get your foot in the door here without having to work for a typical eikaiwa or dispatch company first. But understand that since prior teaching experience is generally required, it's more of a program for ESL teachers considering a transition to Japan from other foreign countries. If you've only just graduated from university yourself then Westgate is probably not a realistic option.

International School Teacher

This is a very different type of job and experience from typical English teaching. It's more like becoming a regular teacher at a public or private school back home, only this time in Japan. That means that international schools aren't just looking for English teachers but people who can teach math, science, history, etc. In most cases you'll need an actual teaching license (not just a TOEFL or CELTA). Specific requirements depend on the individual school and position, but most international schools in Japan seem to require at least a couple years of experience prior to coming here.

Taking the strict requirements into consideration, the salary is naturally going to be a lot higher than that of a typical English teacher. Again, a lot depends on the school, position, and how much experience you have, but an international school teacher can earn a monthly salary in the range of ¥300,000 - ¥700,000. Getting subsidized housing is not uncommon either. Applications are generally accepted either from abroad or from within Japan, but expect the process to take from several months to a year.

5

CELL PHONES, BANK ACCOUNTS

AND OTHER GENERAL INFO

In this chapter you'll find general information on getting set up in Japan. I go over living in a share house, paying taxes, getting a cell phone, obtaining a driver's license and setting up a local bank account. Understand that before doing things like getting a cell phone or opening a bank account, you'll already need to have a valid visa and Residence Card. Searching for accommodation, on the other hand, is something you can start as soon as you arrive.

Short Term Accommodation

Share Houses

If you're here on a budget with no job, you'll need to find a cheap place to stay that won't require you to have a visa. Unless you have Japanese friends willing to put you up for awhile, one of your only options would be a share house. Share houses are especially convenient because they come completely furnished. Furthermore, things like gas, electricity, water and wifi are included in your monthly rent. Most companies require nothing more than your passport and deposit of around ¥30,000. Depending on the company, you may get this deposit back when you move out provided you took decent care of your room.

At a share house you typically have your own room but the kitchen, bathrooms and living area are all communal. Share houses vary greatly in size. My one (and only) share house experience was in a small traditional Japanese-style house built for one small family. The company that renovated it put in rooms for 8 individuals, all of us sharing a single shower and tiny kitchen space. As you can probably imagine, this was not the most comfortable living environment. I lived right next to the kitchen and tiny common area and I could clearly hear most conversations from my room. I could only shower at night because I never knew whether or not the shower would be vacant at all in the mornings. My room was so small that what little floor space I had was occupied by my suitcase and bags, meaning I could only change clothes while standing on top of my bed!

Why did I choose to live in such a place? Basically, I was just in a hurry to find anywhere to stay after spending over a week at a generous friend's apartment. Also, the location was excellent. Later on I ended up visiting another share house that was much larger than where I lived, with a spacious living area, large sofa, wide kitchen and even multiple laundry machines - albeit in a much less convenient part of the city. If I had to do it over again I'd definitely choose something larger than where I ended up.

Some share house companies, such as Sakura House, exclusively target foreigners but others target local Japanese. The whole concept of living in a share house has recently become popular amongst Japanese and now it's quite common for locals on a budget to choose one over a regular apartment.

If you don't mind not being able to see where you're going to live in person before you sign the agreement, Sakura House and other similar companies allow you to book online. The turnover rate at these places are very high, however, so it shouldn't be incredibly difficult to find a decent room within several days of arrival in the country.

Some people see living in a share house as a temporary thing until they can get a job and save up enough money to move into a place of their own. Others actually prefer living in share houses because it means they always have someone to hang out with. I've known foreigners who continued to live in a share house even after having worked in Japan for years. Even if you prefer living alone, you may still want to consider temporarily living in a share house as an alternative to company housing. I go over some of the reasons for this in the next chapter.

Leopalace 21

If you have a little bit more money to spend, you may also want to look into living in a Leopalace 21. These are apartments which you get to live in by yourself and also come fully furnished. You won't have to pay the usual key money and gift money for the landlord, though you will have to pay a deposit. There are various types of contracts, including those that allow you to rent on a month-by-month basis. Be aware that some apartments may require you to have a Japanese guarantor while others may even require you to have your Residence Card already.

The shorter contracts with less commitment required will often come with a higher monthly price. Leopalace is not always the most economical option but it does allow you to avoid the grueling process of renting an apartment here the normal way. Such places also come in handy if you're not sure how much longer you're going to be in the country. The web site of Leopalace allows you to make inquiries in English if you have any specific questions. For details on the typical apartment rental procedure in Japan, skip ahead to Chapter 10.

Airbnb

At one point in time, Airbnb listings were mainly hosted by people that were traveling for a month or two and wanted to sublet their homes out to temporary visitors. Nowadays, however, Airbnb and similar sites like HomeAway are almost exclusively used by hosts looking to make a profit. Therefore, you're unlikely to find anything nearly as affordable as a share house for a long term stay. I'd only recommend Airbnb as an alternative to a regular hotel. When you first arrive in the country, try booking a room on there for a week and use that as your base from which to hunt for a share house.

Paying Taxes

Japan has two types of taxes: income tax and a local tax that you pay to your city or ward, also referred to as "resident's tax." If you're a full-time employee then there's not too much you need to do or worry about, as your employer will automatically withhold income tax from your salary. Japan has a progressive income tax rate. On a typical teacher's salary about 10% will be withheld from your paycheck every month.

It's unlikely that you'll need to file a tax return (*kakutei shinkoku*) yourself as a full-time employee, but that changes if you have more than one job. If you do need to file, do so in between February 16th and March 16th of the following year. While I recommend being compliant, Japan is fairly lenient in regards to late filings. I forgot to file once and a couple months later I received a reminder in the mail. I went ahead and filed and there were no problems after that.

Regarding the resident's tax, you'll receive bills in the mail from your ward or city office after having lived in Japan for a year or more. The amount is based on your total salary from the previous year. These are paid in quarterly installments and each bill will have a due date written on it, easily payable in cash at any convenience store. If you have a hard time paying your taxes when they're due, head over to your local ward or city office and let them know. They won't reduce the total amount of taxes that you owe, but they can break things down for you into smaller monthly payments. Be careful, though, because once they start sending the monthly bills it's not uncommon for them to mess up and continue to send you late notices for the larger quarterly ones. If this happens, head over to the office again to clear things up. If you have any specific questions about taxes or filing a return, contact someone at your company who will likely be able to help out.

Getting a Cell Phone

A cell phone is probably something you're going to need to wait for until after you get your job, your visa and your Residence Card. However, if you already have some Japanese friends then you could find someone kind enough to set up a phone plan for you under their own name. It's not so difficult later on to return to the shop and get the contract switched over to your name. That's what I did when I first came here to job hunt on a tourist visa. Having a way for companies to call me over the phone was really convenient. This plan is somewhat risky though, as if you fail to find a job and need to cancel the plan then you'll be stuck with a hefty cancellation fee.

It's possible to rent a phone but the rental plans were made only with short-term tourists in mind. You may have to pay between ¥1,000 and ¥2,000 per day just to rent a smartphone! If you're going to be spending a couple months job-hunting, paying that much is simply unreasonable.

If you already have an unlocked smart phone, look

into getting a prepaid SIM card. The SIM cards available here are for data only, and it's actually illegal for companies in Japan to provide SIM's with local phone numbers for short-term visitors. As the amount of foreign visitors continues to increase, more and more new SIM card providers are popping up these days. It's best to do your own research before coming, but you may want to check out companies like eConnect or BMobile which have very competitive prices and plans.

If you get ahold of a data SIM card, I recommend you download the app called LINE. Nearly everyone in Japan uses it and it's quite similar to apps like WhatsApp or Viber. You can make free phone calls through LINE as long as you have a data plan or if your phone is connected to a wireless connection. I've never tried this, but perhaps you could share your LINE ID with the companies you're sending applications to as a way for them to call you. Be aware that when you connect with someone over LINE they automatically see your profile picture, so be sure to choose one carefully!

Once you get your Residence Card and are able to sign up for a normal cell phone plan, the major carriers won't let you use your phone brought from home, unfortunately. They'll make you buy a cell phone from one of their shops before allowing you to sign up for a plan. Conversely, if you're switching over from one Japanese carrier to another, using the same phone shouldn't be a problem, so it's basically a matter of Japanese protectionism. It's a major pain but that's just the way Japan works. Another frustrating thing is that as soon as a new model comes out, they stop selling any older models, preventing you from saving money by getting an older phone. Your new phone is usually free at first but must be paid off in monthly installments.

The three major carriers in Japan are SoftBank, AU and Docomo. SoftBank used to be the only company to carry iPhones but now the other companies do as well, so there's really not much of a difference between them anymore. If you're a student, AU is known for giving generous student discounts. Otherwise, I'd recommend just going with the company that has a store closest to where you live. The plans can get confusing so try visiting with a Japanese friend if possible. In reaction to the popularity of apps like LINE, many companies are now including unlimited free domestic calling as part of their basic plans.

Wifi

Bear in mind that wifi access in Japan is horrible and it can be nearly impossible to get connected once you leave your apartment. While the free wifi situation is somewhat improving, Japan is still a decade or so behind the rest of the developed world. Don't be tricked by all the "wifi available" signs you might see on the windows of budget restaurant chains. If you ask the waiter, they'll tell you that you already need to be a subscriber of a particular internet company and if you are, you need to provide some long password the company supposedly gave you when you signed up. Naturally, nobody walks around with this info so it's always baffled me why these restaurants even bother.

There are a now a lot of companies offering rentable pocket wifi devices. These are just like regular modems/wifi routers but in a single pocket-sized device. You can take one with you all over the city and use wifi just as if you were at home. Daily rental fees can get expensive so make sure you can afford it on your budget while you're still job hunting. Later on, once you have a job and move into your own place, I recommend signing up for a monthly pocket wifi plan, as it's usually just as fast and as cheap as a regular modem.

Driving in Japan

If you're going to be living in central Tokyo or Osaka, you don't want or need a car. Parking is hard to come by, not to mention incredibly expensive. The public transport systems are more than enough to get you around. If you'll be living or working in a more rural area then you might want to consider getting a vehicle. If you're an ALT in a small town, your employer may even require it.

For up to one year you can legally drive in Japan with an International Driving Permit. This should be obtained in your home country before coming over. According to Japan Guide, "Japan only recognizes international driving permits based on the 1949 Geneva Convention, which are issued by a large number of countries." People who can't obtain permits recognized by Japan need to get a Japanese driver's license right from the start.[6]

Citizens of many countries can easily get official licenses here as long as they have a valid license back home.

Some examples are Canada, Ireland, Australia and the United Kingdom, among many others. You'll need to get your license translated at your local Japan Automobile Federation (JAF) office which should cost around ¥3,000. Also bring your passport, Residence Card and some proof that your license has been valid for 3 months or longer. After an eye and physical test you should be able to obtain a license without any further visits.[7]

Unfortunately for US citizens, you actually have to take the driving test. This is because US licenses are issued by each state rather than by the federal government, and Japan can't really be bothered to set up a program with each and every state. Even if you'll be taking the test, you need to get your state license translated and bring the proper documents over to the JAF like everyone else. You can then set up an appointment for the driving test.

The actual test will likely consist of a course with many curves and you'll be requested to change lanes, apply the breaks and park while making sure to check your blind spots. It's actually pretty common for people to fail on their first or second tries. Some foreigners have even complained of discrimination, saying that their instructor refused to pass them despite admitting that no mistakes had been made. Discrimination or not, even many Japanese take the test several times before finally passing.

If your company requires that you have a car for your job, they'll likely provide you with a company car and possibly cover some of the costs. They should also give you information on insurance and what to do in case of an accident. Depending on your situation, you may or may not need to cover the fuel costs yourself.

Setting up a Bank Account

When setting up a bank account, you'll need to show the bank some basic identification like your Residence Card and possibly passport. There are some banks where this is all you need, although most banks will require a *hanko/ inkan*, or official stamp. A *hanko* is Japan's equivalent to the signature, and even in this day and age, simply signing your name won't do in certain situations here. To get one, you can go to a local *hanko* shop and have one made with your name in katakana for a few thousand yen. In my case, I've lived here for a long time without ever using one and I've been fine.

Shinsei Bank

The bank most popular with foreigners in Japan is Shinsei Bank. Shinsei does not require a *hanko* and is one of the few banks where a signature is enough. While many holders of other bank cards in Japan are charged fees for basic ATM withdrawals, Shinsei account holders are not. You can use your Shinsei Bank card to withdraw cash from any 7-11, most Family Marts and many Lawson convenience stores for free, 24 hours a day. Post office ATM's are also free.

Online banking, believe it or not, is still quite uncommon here. This is another reason to choose Shinsei, which provides online banking and in English, too. When you set up an account you'll receive a special security card with a unique set of numbers and letters. Before logging into your account you'll be asked to produce a sequence of three letters or numbers found on particular points of the grid on your card.

Be aware that while Shinsei account holders have easy access to ATM's all around the country, actual physical branches are mostly limited to large cities. However, according to their web site, it seems possible to set up an account by mail as long as you send them the proper documents.

Shinsei, as well as some of the other major banks in Japan, allows you to keep money stored in a variety of different currencies but it's not possible to withdraw cash from your foreign currency accounts. Let's say you've received a payment from Europe and now have Euro in your Shinsei account. When you visit Europe and use your Shinsei card to withdraw from the ATM there, the Euro that comes out will actually have been converted and deducted from your Japanese yen account. It seems like the only point of being able to keep money in different currencies is to take advantage of favorable exchange rates. Ultimately, you must convert everything to yen before you withdraw the cash, although you can send foreign currencies via wire transfer.

In conclusion, I can't really think of any reasons *not* to choose Shinsei Bank, unless you're setting up a corporate account. Another option many foreigners choose is a bank account through the national post office, Japan Post.

'My Number' and Foreign Transactions

As of January 2016, many banks, including Shinsei, are requiring customers' 12-digit 'My Number' ID's before allowing anyone to either send or receive money from abroad. The My Number ID and bank accounts were not supposed to be linked until 2018, when even domestic transactions will require the number. With no advance warning, the 2016 policy was suddenly announced at the beginning of the year which came as a shock to many.

But what exactly is 'My Number'? All residents, foreigners included, have been assigned a special number whether they like it or not. This single number is now one's identification number for anything related to their taxes, health insurance and pension payments. There's even been talk of linking one's health checkup and vaccination history with the number. Seriously, that's not a joke. In the past, a person had a separate number for all of these things. Now, any worker at city hall can look up your 'My Number' and learn all sorts of personal information about you.

People have many concerns about this program. Japan is known for having weak IT security and in mid-2015 the pension system was hacked into, resulting in over a million people's personal data getting leaked. Not too long after that, the health insurance database got hacked into as well.[8] There's no reason to believe that cybersecurity is going to improve anytime soon.

Aside from the threat of hackers, the program is disturbing enough even if all goes smoothly and according to plan. Japan has the highest debt to GDP ratio of any country in the world.[9] As the workforce dwindles and the country refuses to accept more immigrants into its labor force, I imagine that the government is going to try its best to plunder as much as it can from the remaining middle class. Even as everyone's pension money is being gambled away with on the foreign stock market, I expect much stricter monitoring of pension payments from here on, not to mention higher taxes and increased capital controls.

For those wishing to send money home every month, it's possible that this could attract the government's attention, as Japan tries to tax the foreign assets of all their residents. Once you're on their radar they could then easily check to see that all your other payments are up to date. If they decide that you owe them something, it's possible a bureaucrat somewhere could just remove that money from your account with a few clicks of a mouse. The system is still brand new and I could be totally wrong about this, but I think it's safe to say that the days of financial privacy in Japan are officially over.

Japanese banks have almost nonexistent interest rates and it's also a very safe country, so keeping cash around may be a good idea. Taking cash home during your next visit is probably a better idea than an international wire. You can legally take any amount under ¥1,000,000 in cash with you on an international flight without needing to declare it to customs. Also be sure to check the amount of cash you're allowed to bring into your destination country.

FATCA

If you're a US citizen and are moving to a foreign

country for the first time, you probably want to do some research on a fairly recently passed law called FATCA, or the Foreign Account Tax Compliance Act. With the passing of FATCA, banks all around the world must now share information about their US account holders with the IRS. All Japanese banks now require US citizens or green card holders to fill out a W-9 or W-8EN form before letting them open an account. These forms ask for your US Social Security Number along with other info.

It's unclear at this point how much information Japanese banks are actually sharing voluntarily with the IRS. I've heard that the banks will only take the initiative to share your info if you have the equivalent of over $50,000 USD in there, but who really knows? You're also legally required yourself to let the IRS know if you have over $10,000 in any foreign bank at any given point in the year. You really might want to consider investing in a good safe after finding a stable job here.

6

SURVIVING YOUR TEACHING JOB

Ok, I know we've just spent a lot of time going over all the steps you need to take to secure a teaching position and a valid working visa. If you haven't started the process or been offered a position yet, some of the things you're about to read in this chapter might scare you off. "Why would I ever want to get myself involved in this?" you may ask yourself. Unfortunately, due to visa restrictions and other factors, there's likely very little else that you can do here in the beginning. In later chapters I'll get more into some of the other opportunities out there beyond teaching. But for now you're probably just going to have to grit your teeth and bear your teaching job for a year or two.

Maybe you'll be one of the lucky few who ends up with an honest company and a friendly boss and at an easygoing school. I really hope things end up working out that way for you. In any case, it's best to mentally prepare yourself for some of the potential issues you could encounter at these jobs so you can prevent yourself from getting caught off guard if they do occur.

What's So Bad About Eikaiwa?

Teaching English at a private conversation school sounds like a simple and relatively fulfilling job on paper. Could the job and lifestyle really be as bad as people say on internet forums or down at the local Hub? Students pay the school money and you teach them English. The school pays you a livable wage with which you're able to cover the bills and have fun on the weekends. You watch your students' skills progress and you come home every night satisfied that you've made a positive impact on another person's life. Sounds like a pretty decent gig, right? It should be, but unfortunately the job rarely works out so smoothly in reality.

First of all, you need to understand that there's a big gap between the amount of money students pay the school and the salary that the school pays their teachers. The students pay a lot of money for each lesson and have very high expectations. They have no idea that their teacher is getting paid roughly $1/4^{th}$ of what they're shelling out. Teachers are often overworked and sometimes can't even do their jobs properly because of all the communication issues that are so prevalent at eikaiwa schools. It's only natural that students are not always going to get the quality of lessons they expect.

Poor efforts by the Japanese staff to communicate with foreign teachers is a much too common issue in the industry. It's normal for a branch manager to withhold important details from you until the very last minute and for no apparent reason. For example, you may not hear that a student is quitting until the day of their last lesson, or that even though you've already planned your next lesson with one of your younger students, you're suddenly informed that their mother has chosen a new text book. "When was this decided?" you may ask. "Oh, sometime last week," the branch manager tells you. Don't be surprised if you're always the last one to learn important details - information that you need to effectively carry out the very job they're paying you to do!

Other communication issues include the staff not telling you about students' complaints. Maybe you get along well enough with a certain student but they've been expecting a different style of lesson. These are often very minor things, such as you having spent too much time with free conversation practice instead of the workbook, or vice versa. The student will almost never tell you this directly because Japan is an incredibly indirect culture. In Japanese society, a lot of communication, especially complaints or bad news, goes through a third or even fourth party before it finally reaches the intended recipient. Surely the school secretary or branch manager will let you know about these minor complaints so you can adjust your lessons accordingly, right? Well no, they often won't. Sometimes the students complain about a minor problem for *months* without the school ever mentioning a single thing to the teacher. Basic courtesy aside, withholding such information from teachers makes absolutely no sense from a business perspective.

Branch managers also commonly mess up the

scheduling, both on the students' and teachers' ends. It's not uncommon for a student not on your schedule that day to suddenly show up for their "lesson" during your assigned lunch break. To save face, the branch manager might even try to get you to skip lunch and teach them.

There are also a number of problems with being an eikaiwa teacher that fall on the students themselves. In Japan, where appearance, presentation and playing roles are so important, the students at eikaiwa are often looking for a teacher that fits their ideal image of a foreigner. If you've ever watched Japanese TV or commercials, you may have an idea of what this stereotypical image is - very smiley, energetic and *genki*. Many Japanese students are more concerned with how well their teachers fit into the "*genki* foreigner" stereotype than with how well they can teach. Constantly putting on this fake persona can become incredibly tiresome, especially on days where you're teaching for around 6 hours straight.

You may also notice that some older students seem to be using the lessons as some kind of therapy session. A housewife might go on and on in explicit detail about their sick family member or dying pet, week after week, month after month. Then they might even complain to the staff that you're not smiley and *genki* enough during their lessons!

Mothers of your younger students will complain when their children's grades aren't improving. Never mind the fact that their child only shows up every other lesson and hardly ever does their homework. The family is paying lots of money and expect concrete results, as if language ability were a luxury item that could be obtained with enough cash. If the parents then take their kid away from the school, management will often blame the teacher.

Some students may quit for reasons that have nothing to do with you, but with the school itself. The company might pressure students into buying books directly from them for over ¥20,000 when the same book could easily be found on Amazon for ¥2,000. I've even had students complain to me that the company was dishonest about their makeup lesson policy, screwing them out of lessons they'd been promised. When the students/customers become aware of these shady business practices and quit the school, the teacher gets blamed yet again.

Some companies will keep detailed records of all the students that their teachers "lost" over the year, which they might use to confront you with. Your boss might show you this data one day, nothing but a list of numbers without any names or explanations listed. When business is going bad they'll need one or multiple scapegoats for that particular branch's poor performance. Never mind the fact that the company raised their prices that year, or the staff messed up the students' scheduling multiple times, or talked the students into buying too many overpriced books. The company will try to convince the teachers they're somehow responsible for all of this. I've had several students quit a school that I was working at only for them to contact me privately to see if I could teach them at a coffee shop. Meanwhile, my boss was trying to have me believe that those same students quit because something was wrong with me or my teaching.

Then there are the downright illegal and immoral practices that many employers in the industry are infamous for. I've had one company force entire days of unpaid overtime on all their teachers. They finally abolished the practice, but only for those teachers that agreed to give up their yearly contract completion bonuses. Those that refused to give up their bonuses were stuck with even more unpaid overtime. I've also had a company suddenly tell me that one of the branches I was working at was shutting down and they had nowhere else to put me. Despite my full-time contract and predetermined salary, they told me they'd have to start paying me part-time wages instead.

Companies will also typically not let you use your vacation days when you want to. Let's say you've been working hard for many months and want to take 5 of your annual paid leave days to relax on the beach in Thailand. Your employer will probably only allow you to take one or two days off at a time. One way to get around this without causing a lot of drama is to make up a story about a sick relative you need to go visit back home, and then head off to your tropical destination instead. It's a shame that making up stories is necessary to take the vacation days you're entitled to by law.

If you look through internet forums and read some personal accounts of other eikaiwa teachers, many have experienced much worse treatment than I have. I can't validate the authenticity of everything people write on the internet but I do find many of these stories believable.

To be fair, there are many companies that operate all over the country. Even within a single company there may be multiple branches, each with its own unique set of students and staff. Not all teachers have a terrible experience with eikaiwa. I've met some people who genuinely enjoy their jobs, and on the positive end of my own experiences, I've had some great students that I looked forward to teaching every week. I also did get along well with many of the secretaries and even some of the branch managers at schools where I worked.

Even if you're lucky enough to work for a good school without communication issues and where everyone gets along, you still want to get out of eikaiwa as soon as you can. The longer you stay in eikaiwa, the dimmer your chances of finding other work becomes, whether within Japan or back in your own country. Sure, one or two years teaching English in an exotic culture can impress a prospective employer back home, but 4 or 5 years of it will look like a big black hole on your resume. Time flies by extremely quickly in Japan and before you know it your contract will be up for renewal already. I've seen many teachers sign new contracts after promising themselves they'd just continue for one more year. The next thing they know, several years have already flown by.

For those intending to stay in Japan long-term, understand that your salary will hardly every increase no matter how long you're with your eikaiwa company. There are a lot of people trying to come over here every year, giving companies little incentive to raise the salaries of their experienced teachers when they could just replace them with a fresh face. If you end up as a 32-year-old teacher with 10 years of experience, you'll still be earning roughly the same amount as a 22-year-old who's just stepped off the plane.

Many single teachers feel their pay is good enough because they can get by paying rent and still have some money left over to get drunk on the weekends. After starting families, however, they panic when it finally hits them that they'll be on the same entry-level salary forever. I'm not trying to sound condescending but I've just witnessed so many teachers get stuck in a rut here and I'm only trying to keep you informed. To put it simply, eikaiwa is fine for a year or two adventure but it was never meant to be a career.

Eikaiwa companies that you should thoroughly research before applying to: GABA,[10] Shane,[11] CoCo Juku[12] and WinBe,[13] among others.

What's So Bad About Being an ALT?

A lot of the problems associated with being a dispatch ALT are a result of the way the industry as a whole operates. First of all, there's a serious lack of job security, even when compared to eikaiwa. Your local Board of Education (BoE) might suddenly decide they don't want any ALT's in their town next semester, or they might just sign an agreement with a different dispatch company. No matter how hard you work or how close your relationship becomes with the staff at your school, your job could just suddenly vanish at any moment.

These days, the BoE's are constantly on the lookout for the cheapest prices. If a new company comes along that's offering the school district a lower price than what your employer is offering, you're pretty much screwed. Interac, the largest ALT dispatch company in Japan, is well-known for undercutting the competition. As prices offered to the BoE's get lower and lower, it's only natural for teachers' salaries to go down as well. Despite the ESL industry standard being at around ¥250,000 per month, it's not uncommon these days to find full-time ALT positions starting at ¥230,000, ¥210,000 and even down to ¥180,000 per month! These wages are simply unlivable in present-day Japan.

Furthermore, a lot of these companies are deliberately vague when it comes to how much pay their ALT's will receive during the winter and summer breaks. Be sure to confirm these details with your company before signing any new contract. If you're not going to get paid then you'll need to look for some kind of short-term gig during your time off. Some of the better dispatch companies do actually pay full salaries for their teachers when school isn't in session, although that's becoming increasingly rare.

Aside from issues with the dispatch companies themselves, the overall school environment can make ALT work a soul-crushing experience. Even if you've been living in Japan for a little while already, many aspects of the Japanese education system may shock you. For one, there's hardly any disciplinary action taken at all. No detentions, no suspensions and no removal of a problem child from the classroom so that other students can concentrate. As a foreign ALT, your contract bars you from intervening in any scuffle or dispute between students aside from just telling kids to be quiet. If stuck in a classroom with a problem child, you're forced to endure constant disruptions. Things can become very uncomfortable when you witness obvious bullying going on right in front of everyone as the

Japanese English teacher (JTE) chooses to ignore it.

Every so often there are major news stories in Japan about young students that commit suicide. If it wasn't due to extreme pressure to pass a major exam, it's often revealed that these children were heavily bullied at school. The typical reaction from that school administration is to deny that they ever had any way of knowing about the bullying. Having worked at a Japanese school, however, I can say that most of the bullying is done very much out in the open while the school administration does absolutely nothing about it. For me, this was by far the most difficult part of the job. Despite it being very clear that certain kids were suffering, it was against my contract to interfere or get involved in any significant way. The best I could do was make an extra effort to be friendly with those students when I saw them in the hallways or after class.

One time during a lesson I was reading a vocabulary list out loud (in my typical "human tape recorder" role) when a student from an entirely different class suddenly walked into the room and smacked his usual bullying victim right in the back of the head! In shock, I stopped reading but the JTE told me to continue on as if nothing had happened. The JTE calmly told the bully to return to his own classroom, but no punishment was dished out for the violence and no comfort whatsoever was offered to the victim. This is only one of many such examples.

In another instance, that same teacher himself even got into a physical altercation with a student as I was reading a long essay. The 12-year-old had the 60-something-year-old man in an arm lock, but then the teacher reversed it and got the student in an arm lock of his own! The kid was howling in pain as the JTE told me "It's ok, don't mind. Just keep reading." They continued to scuffle right next to me for another couple of minutes. I was actually on pretty good terms with this teacher, and when we talked about it later in the staff room he just laughed it off. No punishment was ever administered to the student (or to the teacher).

Meanwhile, students in Japan seem to get screamed at for the tiniest little things, like wearing their uniform incorrectly or being slightly late to an assembly. But if that same student hits another classmate, or vandalizes their own desk with the words "Suzuki-sensei is a *hentai*"? Nobody bats an eye, at least not where I worked. I understand that the school I worked at was in an especially bad town and many of the students were the children of the local gangsters (yes, you read that correctly). If you get stuck in a bad school it's usually out of the control of your employer and this could happen to you even as a JET. As I mentioned, there are so many variables involved with ALT work that it's difficult to make too many generalizations about the job. On a positive note, I worked once a week at an elementary school in the same town. The students, staff and overall atmosphere was so much better there and I looked forward to those days each week.

Like eikaiwa, ALT work was never meant to be a career. Despite disliking the overall environment, I actually did form pretty good relationships with the other teachers and staff and they gave my employer positive feedback about me. All of a sudden, however, the prefectural BoE decided they didn't need any ALT's for the next semester. While they were not going to switch dispatch companies, they now only wanted foreign teachers for two-thirds of the year so they could cut costs. When the second semester ended I had to look for a new job all over again. Getting a dispatch ALT job is a great way to get your first visa, but I wouldn't see it as much more than that.

Dispatch companies that you should thoroughly research before applying to: Interac,[14] Heart,[15] RCS[16] and Borderlink,[17] among others.

The *Shakai Hoken* Controversy

In Japan, companies that employ full-time workers are required by law to provide something known as *shakai-hoken*. This is a combination of national health insurance and pension, of which the company pays half and automatically deducts the other half from their employees' paychecks every month. In regards to eikaiwa and dispatch ALT companies, the whole *shakai hoken* issue is a very controversial one because most of these companies break the law by refusing to pay for it.

The minimum weekly number of hours that one has to work before their employer is required to pay for *shakai hoken* is thirty. Even though teachers, either at public schools or eikaiwa, are at work for 8 or 9 hours a day, companies will carefully adjust their teachers' schedules so that the total teaching hours don't exceed 29.5 hours per week. Obviously, this is a big scam because your working hours don't only consist of the time you're teaching and you're often not even allowed to leave the school when you don't have a lesson. These companies have been getting away with this for years and years and will likely continue to do so.

You may not necessarily want to be paying into the *shakai hoken* system, however. Without that money being taken out of your paycheck every month you'd be making a significantly higher salary. Furthermore, if you're not planning to retire in Japan, paying into the pension system is a total waste. Even if you are planning to retire here, paying pension is likely a waste as the government gambles with everyone's pension money on the foreign stock market. For some nationalities it's possible to get most of the pension money back when you leave, but only up to 3 years' worth.

If you get hired by a company that does insist on you joining the *shakai hoken* system (most don't but some do), there won't be much at all taken out during your first year. That's because the amount you pay is based on your previous year's salary. Since in your first year this would amount to zero, the health insurance will be especially cheap. From the second year, however, *shakai hoken* can start to make a big dent in your paycheck. On a typical English teacher's salary you can expect to have ¥30,000 - ¥40,000 taken out every month.

There's another type of national health insurance in Japan called *kokumin hoken*. This is insurance that you apply for by yourself at your city office (*shiyakusho* or *kuyakusho*) and works in much the same way. *Kokumin hoken* is intended for self-employed or part-time workers, and if your employer decides that you only work 29.5 hours per week, then you are technically part-time. On either type of health insurance plan you still have to pay 30% of the total cost of each visit to a hospital or clinic.

Personally, I find the national healthcare plans to be overpriced, especially considering how affordable the upfront costs for health services are in Japan. Japanese people tend to visit the doctor or hospital whenever they catch even a minor cold. That's probably why many locals find the system to be a good value. From my experience, I've saved a lot by not paying into the national insurance system and by only visiting a doctor a few times a year. I even needed some physical therapy recently but a single session at my local clinic cost just ¥1,500 without insurance. I've also had minor dermatologic surgery and paid only a little over ¥20,000 for it upfront. In case of a major emergency, I have affordable private insurance from abroad that covers me over here.

So is this practice by ESL companies of breaking the law to save some yen every month shady? Absolutely, yes. But are you going to be worse off because of it? Not necessarily. Some companies will actually give you the option of whether or not you want to be on it. If you have a family in Japan, you'll want to be receiving *shakai hoken*. For a slight extra fee per month your non-working family members will also be covered by your plan. If you're single and don't intend to live here permanently then I wouldn't recommend signing up for it. Don't just listen to me, though. If given the opportunity to choose, do your own research before making a decision.

You should also be aware that many eikaiwa companies who don't allow their employees to enroll in *shakai hoken* nonetheless require them to have some kind of private insurance. They sometimes have their own insurance programs which are a rip-off, similar to how they rent out apartments to teachers at higher rates. If you just tell your company that you already have some kind of insurance then they might not even ask you to prove it. If you want to avoid joining the company's program, look for alternative cheaper insurance here or some kind of insurance from your home country that covers you internationally.

Things may be changing from October 2016, as the laws are about to become more strict. The minimum number of working hours required for one to receive the *shakai hoken* benefits will be lowered down to twenty.[18] Only time will tell how most eikaiwa and dispatch companies react to the new requirements, but it's possible that things could get even worse. Some companies are already taking action by changing their teachers' status from 'employee' to 'subcontractor.' Should this practice be adopted by most companies in the future, it could potentially result in even less, or possibly no benefits or protection at all!

Understand that once you join the national health insurance or pension programs and then take a break, you'll be expected to back pay if you rejoin the system again later. My first employer in Japan actually provided *shakai hoken* while my second employer did not. Halfway through my second job, I inquired about *kokumin hoken* at my local ward office and was told I'd have to back pay a significant amount without getting anything in return. Since then I've never rejoined the system and have been fine. I've renewed my visa any number of times without ever being asked to show proof of insurance or pension payments. Were I to eventually apply for something like permanent residency, however, this inconsistency would probably cause a lot of complications. If being part of the national insurance and pension programs actually do become requirements for visa renewals in the future, it's best to be fully compliant from the very beginning if you can.

Company Accommodation

Before starting your new job, your company may give the option of living in company accommodation. Considering how expensive and difficult it is for foreigners to rent their own apartments (as will be discussed in a later chapter) accepting company housing might sound like a good idea. If you've been hired prior to arriving in Japan then you may not even have any choice in the matter at all.

While moving into company accommodation won't require you to pay the exorbitant deposits and "gift money" that you would to a normal landlord in Japan, you'll most likely be paying higher rent than the other tenants in your building. If you're working in Tokyo, for example, don't be surprised to be stuck living in the suburbs but paying central Tokyo rent. This is another way these English companies make a profit. Consequently, teachers living in company housing tend to get treated better. If there's a problem at your school or branch, you might just get left alone as long as the company can keep making money by having you as a tenant.

On the other hand, let's say that you do have a problem or a serious dispute with your employer somewhere down the road. You won't have much leverage considering the fact that your employer also controls your living situation. Suddenly becoming unemployed is bad enough, but losing your job and apartment at the same time would be a total disaster. You also don't want to feel you have to keep working for a shady employer just out of concern for your housing situation.

From my experience here, I would never feel comfortable with an employer having control over my living situation, unless it was through a program like JET. There's just too much that could go wrong at once. For this reason, I recommend living in a share house or Leopalace when you first get here. If you plan to live in Japan for over a year, then as painful as the process may be, it's a good idea to rent an apartment under your own name once you have the cash. Chapter 10 is entirely dedicated to this process.

Joining a Union

Considering the rampant abuses of workers' rights and disregard for labor laws by many eikaiwa and dispatch companies, some people may want to consider joining a union. I've never been part of a union in Japan myself. However, as I mentioned earlier, there was a time when one of my employers tried to change the conditions of my contract and salary halfway through the year. I didn't know where to turn to for help or what I could do to fight it. Just as I was about to contact a lawyer for advice, the problem luckily resolved itself, as the company suddenly found another branch to place me. But I learned that you don't really know if you'll need help until after something bad actually happens. Consulting a lawyer or looking up labor laws in the Japanese language can be very stressful and overwhelming so you may want to consider joining a union in advance. One of the big unions that many teachers join is simply called the General Union.

In their own words:

We are a legally registered labor union in Japan which is open to all nationalities. Formed in 1991, we have built a strong reputation by protecting workers' rights and improving working conditions. The General Union is a group of workers who support each other for the benefit of all. Please note that we are not a cheap legal service, and that you need to join the Union [. . .] if you wish to receive its help and advice.[19]

Some opponents of joining a union say that your employer could find some way to pressure you or fire you indirectly after discovering that you've joined. It's best to keep your affiliation a secret and only get the union involved when necessary. Others argue that it's not worth it for short-term teachers to join a union, as a lawsuit could potentially take years. However, in the best-case scenario, the union could pressure your employer and settle the issue before it even gets to court, as the company may just want to avoid any bad publicity.

7

UNEMPLOYMENT

Quitting Your Job

If you find a better opportunity than the teaching job you're currently at, don't hesitate to give your notice. I think a lot of teachers make the mistake of feeling guilty about switching jobs, or feel that it would somehow be unethical to not fulfill the entire length of their contract. I used to think this way myself. Looking back, I can't emphasize enough how as a foreigner in Japan, it's very important to concentrate on what's best for you. I'm not talking about being selfish or deliberately doing anything to harm others, and I'm not talking about breaking any laws (leave that to the ESL companies!) I just mean that you need to watch out for yourself because nobody in the ESL industry is looking out for you. Don't worry about how leaving your job wouldn't be very "nice" to your employer. Your boss or supervisor at your company may be very pleasant and friendly, and this could make you feel guilty about quitting. Don't worry about it. Stay at most of these companies long enough and they'll eventually screw you over in one way or another as soon as it's convenient for them. If you find a better job or just can't stand your current one anymore, give the proper amount of notice stipulated by your contract, move on and don't look back.

Regarding your visa situation, Japan is somewhat unique to Asia because according to the law, your visa belongs to you. While you do need a company to sponsor you in the first place, it's the government that approves your visa and grants it to you. Your company has no control over your visa status past the initial sponsorship. This is important to keep in mind because some companies make threats to teachers that want to quit, saying they could revoke their visas if they leave. This is all a bluff. The company does not actually have such power.

There's been a recent change to Japan's visa policy that you need to be aware of, however. In the past, a foreigner could quit their job and the immigration authorities wouldn't really care what they were up to as long as they found a new job and sponsor by the time their visa ran out. For example, if you got a 3 year visa and then quit your job after one year, you could travel for several months and come back to Japan to job hunt without any trouble. Now when a foreigner quits their job, both the foreign individual *and* their employer must inform immigration about it within 2 weeks. After that, the foreign worker must inform immigration within 3 months that they've found a new job.

No visit to the immigration office is required and the forms can easily be sent online via the Immigration Bureau's web site. First you need to register for an account. When informing immigration of your new job, there's nowhere on the form that asks you to state the salary or provide a copy of the contract. The key points are the company name, address and start date. I've done this without any further questioning from immigration. While I did receive an auto confirmation after I sent it, I have no evidence that any human has even looked at the form at all.

This is still a new system and there don't appear to be any reported cases online yet of people who've gotten a warning from immigration after failing to find a new job within 3 months. It's hard to say how strictly this is actually going to be enforced. There's also supposed to be some leeway if you can provide evidence that you've been going to interviews or are at least applying for jobs. Since the form doesn't ask for specific salary information or hours, it seems fine to just get a part-time job somewhere (relevant to your visa) and use that company's info on the form. Things are always changing so I highly recommend researching online or even contacting immigration themselves if you have trouble finding a job before your three months are up.

Collecting Unemployment Insurance

All full-time workers in Japan are required to pay for unemployment insurance (*shitsugyou hoken* or *koyou hoken*) which is automatically taken out of their salary every month. It only amounts to a couple thousand yen or so. If you've been working for over a year total and have been paying unemployment insurance the entire time, you'll be eligible to receive unemployment benefits when you find yourself without a job. Yes, even foreigners can receive this.

There's one major factor when it comes to how soon you can start receiving the benefits: whether you've been fired from your job or if you've quit. If you were fired, you can start receiving benefits right away, provided you've already been working for a year or more up to that point. If you quit, you're still eligible for benefits but only after 3 months of job hunting. If you still haven't found a new job after the 3 months are up, only then can you start receiving the benefits. Bear in mind that if you find a job at any point during the process, it should be possible to receive all of your unreleased insurance money in a lump sum payment.

Simply letting a one-year contract expire and deciding not to renew it is a gray area and you'll need to discuss your situation with someone at your local Hello Work office (ハローワーク), the government agency which handles unemployment issues. When you tell your company that you don't plan to renew your contract, **do not sign anything**. One time my former boss politely asked if I could put my intention to not renew my contract into writing "just for their records." Without thinking, I quickly wrote something down on a blank sheet of paper and gave it to him. Only later, when the next job I thought I had lined up ended up falling through, did I realize that my written statement counted as an official resignation. Due to my carelessness I couldn't receive the insurance money right away.

No matter how bad the split with your former employer is, they are legally required by law to send you a special separation notice called the *rishokuhyo* (離職票) after you stop working for them. Without this document you cannot apply to receive unemployment benefits. If you've never seen a *rishokuhyo* before then you wouldn't know what it's supposed to look like. For this reason, some companies lazily send out simple letters which state you no longer work there. This is not the document you need! This is deceptive and ends up being a bigger waste of everyone's time. If your former employer is being stubborn, have someone from Hello Work call them up and they should get their act together. The frustrating thing is that if the company sends out the *rishokuhyo* late, there's no penalty for them and it just means more waiting time for you.

Once you receive the *rishokuhyo* in the mail, take it along with 2 photographs (3 x 2.5cm), insurance card, bank passbook/card and your Residence Card to your local Hello Work office.[20] There may be a few people there that speak English, but unless your Japanese ability is pretty good it's best to have a native speaker accompany you.

When you first show up at Hello Work they'll ask you some basic information about yourself, such as your work history and any skills you may have. They'll also want to know your Japanese ability. This is information they'll keep on their system to help match you with new jobs that may come up.

You'll also receive a schedule of each time you need to come back to their offices for a meeting or consultation. At each of these meetings you need to prove that you're actively searching for a job. The evidence required to prove this is 4 or 5 special stamps each month. Each Hello Work office has computers containing tons of data on open positions throughout the country. You'll come in, search on the computer and print out several pages of information about jobs that interest you. Then you'll meet with a staff member at the office for a consultation. They'll give you advice on whether or not the positions would be a good fit and after each of these consultations they'll stamp a special sheet of paper that you receive at your first orientation. Regardless of how much of an effort you're putting into your job hunt at home, you still need to keep getting these stamps if you want that insurance money.

The bigger cities have Hello Work offices especially for foreigners but the computer database is the same no matter which office you visit. Everything is in Japanese and there are lots and lots of kanji to get through. Even with my decent language skills I had a really hard time navigating these computers and finding appropriate positions. The consultations, on the other hand, were helpful and informative. Hello Work can introduce you to something outside the realm of teaching or headhunting but the staff don't seem to be experts on working visas for foreigners. They may inadvertently suggest a job that falls outside of what your visa category legally allows you to do.

So how much unemployment insurance can you actually earn? The amount you receive is a certain percentage of your last job's wages, spread out over 3 months. Also, the percentage depends on your age - the older you are the more you receive. The system they use to determine the amount is confusing and I won't get into it here, but the one time I received benefits I was in my 20's and my previous job had paid me ¥275,000 per month. Over the entire period I probably received a total of roughly ¥500,000.

Be careful - if you get caught working while receiving your unemployment benefits, Hello Work can force you to pay them back the amount they paid you three times over! I definitely don't recommend this, but many people do it anyway despite knowing the risks.

Getting unemployment benefits may be trickier now with Japan's new visa policy, since the government doesn't want any foreigner to be unemployed for over 3 months. If you can't find a job within 3 months, it might be possible to receive an extension if you can prove you've been visiting Hello Work the whole time.

Living Frugally

Japan is a very expensive place to live and being unemployed here is rough. You don't have the benefit of moving back to your parents' home like many Japanese do so it's vital to live as frugally as possible. Some of these tips are pretty obvious but here's a short list of things that have helped me out when money was tight:

- Walk or bike as much as possible
- If there's an item you need to buy, check to see if someone's selling it used on Craigslist first
- When buying something new, Amazon.jp is generally cheaper than anything you can find in a physical store
- Check online for flea markets happening near you
- If you have something to get rid of, try selling it on Craigslist or Yahoo! Auction

- If it's winter, wear many layers of clothing inside to avoid getting stuck with a massive electric bill
- There a number of cheap family restaurant chains where only a couple hundred yen gets you unlimited coffee and tea
- Take your computer and work on your resume at these restaurants in the winter or summer to save on AC costs
- Head to the supermarkets late in the evening to get your hands on those 50% off bento boxes or sushi
- Cook!
- Buy cheap *happoshu* instead of beer
- Depending on how close you live to one, you may want to consider a Costco membership. This is a better idea if you live with roommates, as typical Japanese apartments just don't have the storage space for bulk items.

8

ALL ABOUT VISAS

Applying For a Visa Before Arrival in Japan

If you live close to a Japanese consulate or embassy then you might be able to apply for a visa directly. However, this process is often time consuming because it must go through the "Japanese Embassy, then by the Ministry of Foreign Affairs, and finally by [the] Immigration Bureau," according to Acroseed. The process "takes time because the Immigration Bureau decides and replies to the Ministry of Foreign Affairs whether to grant the visa [...]"[21]

A quicker and much more common approach is to apply for what's known as the "Certificate of Eligibility for Status of Residence." With help from your visa sponsor, this process is mainly handled by the nearest Immigration Bureau to wherever you'll be living in Japan and the whole thing can take up to 3 months. You'll receive the Certificate by mail and then you can take it to your nearest Embassy or Consulate to get the visa in about 1 week. When there, they'll expect you to already have your flight booked and may even want to know your flight number. Alternatively, you could also come to Japan with your CoE and change it over to a visa once you're here.

Some of the basic documents required when applying for your CoE/visa are a copy of your university diploma and a copy of your contract with your employer which clearly states your salary and working conditions. You also need certain documents from your employer like a certificate of registry of the company, a withholding tax report and other recent financial statements. Your employer will either send these to you directly or they might just send them to the immigration authorities themselves. Every application process is slightly different but your sponsor should be able to guide you through everything.

Applying for a Visa from Within Japan

If you're in Japan as a tourist and then find a company or school willing to sponsor your visa, it is not necessary to leave Japan to change your residency status. Since the process can take awhile, there may be a situation in which the visa is still being processed after your landing permission / tourist visa has already expired. In these cases they'll give you special permission to remain in the country until everything gets approved.

Overall, the process generally works in much the same way as applying for a visa in your home country. When getting my first visa in Japan, my company was actually headquartered in another city. We communicated via phone and email to make sure all the documents were in order. They sent everything to immigration and then my CoE was approved and sent to me in the mail. I took the certificate to my local immigration office and filled out a new application for the visa. When you're applying from within Japan, you'll usually get a special postcard in the mail once the application has finally been processed. Next, just head over to your nearest immigration office and pick up your shiny new visa and Residence Card.

A few tips:

Visits to the immigration office can be stressful and time consuming. Despite being an office that deals exclusively with foreigners, many of the staff do not speak any English at all. To make matters worse, some of the people there can seem just plain sadistic. I had a guy behind the desk raise his voice at me once just because one little minor detail on a form was off. Another time I was told to go home and come back again with a specific document before they could process my application. After researching online and consulting with my employer, it didn't seem like this was a document that's normally required and it also takes time to obtain. I returned the next day without it and was luckily called up to a different desk. Sure enough, my application was accepted and processed without any problems. It can sometimes feel as if the immigration office was deliberately designed to make foreigners regret their decision to come here. The best you can do is relax, double check that you have everything filled out correctly and consult with your employer when necessary. They've already offered you the position so they're going to do their best to make sure your visa gets approved.

Some companies have lawyers that will take all your documents and visit the immigration office for you. This makes the process so much smoother and stress-free. It also increases your chances of getting a longer visa. Unfortunately, most companies still require you to go there by yourself.

Recent Changes to The System

Japan's immigration system was recently overhauled in 2012. In the past, you would need to get your visa and then visit your local city or ward office to apply for your Alien Registration Card a.k.a. *gaikokujin tourokushou*. This has now been replaced by what's simply known as the Residence Card, or *zairyuu kaado* (在留カード). Instead of your city office, this process is now handled by your regional immigration bureau and you receive it along with your visa. Actually, the Residence Card itself now pretty much *is* your visa, as it's taken the place of what was formerly a stamp in your passport.

If you've already been granted your visa before arrival in Japan, it's apparently possible to receive your Residence Card at the airport. According to Japan Guide, "All new foreign residents are issued a residence card upon initially entering Japan at Narita, Haneda, Kansai or Chubu Airports. New residents arriving through different ports can get their cards at their municipal offices."[22]

Many long-term expats use the terms "gaijin card," "alien card" and "residence card" interchangeably, even though only the latter currently exists. When browsing the internet for information, be sure to check when the information was posted. If it's from before 2012 then any info regarding "alien cards" is out of date.

One major positive change brought by the new Residence Card system is that foreigners no longer need to apply for a re-entry permit every time they want to travel abroad. Now you can freely leave the country and enter Japan again using your Residence Card, as long as you've been gone for under a year.

Another major change is that the maximum visa length has been extended from 3 to 5 years. Getting a 5-year visa as your very first visa in Japan may be unlikely, although I do know a few people who got one straight from a tourist visa. In those cases their company had a lawyer handle all the paperwork for them.

'My Number'

If you receive your visa and residence card after Jan 1st 2016, you will also automatically be issued a 'My Number.' I went over this in detail in Chapter 5, but in summary it's a 12 digit ID number issued to all residents of Japan that links together tax, insurance and pension information. It will also soon be linked to bank accounts and may even contain one's health records in the future. At the time of writing, receiving a special plastic card with your 'My Number' on it is optional. You've still been assigned a number by the government whether you're in possession of the card or not. For tax filing purposes, your employer will likely ask for your number when you start your new job.

Renewing Your Visa

Renewing your visa is not as difficult a process as getting your very first one, but it can still be pretty stressful. If your sponsor is different this time or if you're changing over to a different visa type, things can sometimes get complicated. In any case, similar to getting your first visa, you'll need an application form along with a number of documents provided by your employer.

On your end, you'll need to obtain a document called the *nozei shomei sho* (納税証明書) which is a special certificate that proves you've been paying your taxes. To get this, visit your local city or ward office and tell them you need one for your visa renewal. The process should be pretty straightforward and depending on how crowded the office is, they should be able to prepare one for you in under an hour.

During the same visit to your ward office, also ask them for a *kazei shomei sho* (課税証明書). This is an income certificate. Again, your sponsor should be able to help you out with any specific questions you may have.

If you've moved recently then you may need to

have your current city or ward office contact your old one. Things can get especially complicated if you've moved to another part of the country. You'll probably have to wait for the documents from your previous ward office to arrive in the mail, potentially delaying the entire application process.

Different Types of Visas

The descriptions provided by the government for different visa types can sometimes be incredibly vague, leaving many situations to be determined by officials on a case by case basis. If you have questions about visas in relation to a unique situation, it's best to contact the Ministry of Foreign Affairs directly or hire an immigration lawyer. I am certainly no legal expert.

Just because you have one type of visa it doesn't always mean that you're absolutely barred from doing other types of work. To do so, however, you need special permission from immigration. If you get a part-time offer from a company in another industry while you're already working somewhere else full-time, you can take the part-time contract to immigration to see if they'll grant you permission. Some examples are people taking modeling side-gigs while teaching English, or doing some translation work on top of a computer programming job. The form can be found here: http://www.immi-moj.go.jp/english/tetuduki/kanri/shyorui/09.html

Important note: The Japanese government generally views a minimum salary of ¥200,000 a month as adequate for a foreigner to survive here. To get approved for a visa, make sure your total salary adds up to around this much, whether you have a single full-time job or a combination of different part-time jobs.

Below is a summary of the requirements for some of the most common visa categories in Japan:

Artist Visa

Japan seems to attract many different creative-types and there are likely a lot of people wondering about working here as some kind of artist. According to the Ministry of Foreign Affairs' web site, this visa is for people working as sculptors, photographers, craftspeople, painters or composers, among other jobs.[23]

To be allowed to work full-time as an artist in Japan, one generally must prove at least 10 years experience in their chosen field prior to coming here. This may come as a surprise to those familiar with the visa system of European countries like Germany, for example, where it's easy for most people to get an artist visa even without much experience.

I've heard that there's a ridiculously small amount of Artist Visas granted in Japan every year (under 100), although I haven't been able to confirm this through any official sources.

Cultural Activities Visa

This is not a work visa, but more like another type of student visa. It's for those who wish to study a specific aspect of Japanese culture, such as tea ceremony, ikebana, religion or martial arts. You'll need to choose a field of study and provide the immigration authorities with evidence that you'll be studying with qualified teachers for a certain number of hours every week. You'll also need to prove sufficient funds for living in Japan. Your chances of being approved for this visa largely depend on what you want to study and with whom. Be sure to check with your teacher, instructor, master, or whoever will be overseeing your studies about what you'll need to do to apply.

Dependent Visa

If you have a spouse or family member that's a foreigner working in Japan, you may be able to come here on a Dependent Visa. You'll only be able to work a limited amount of hours per week, usually no more than 28.

Engineer Visa

The Engineer Visa applies to those working as IT engineers, software/web developers or as mechanical engineers. Like other visa types, the applicant will likely need a B.S. in the relevant field or 10 years experience prior to coming to Japan.

Apparently, the Engineer category has recently

been merged with the Specialist in Humanities Visa type, resulting in some kind of mega visa category known as "Engineer/Specialist in Humanities/International Services." It's unlikely that the merger will have any impact on the necessary experience or certifications required to legally do engineer work, however.

Entertainment Visa

This visa is for entertainers and performers and can last from 3 months to a year. Touring musicians or performing artists who come to play shows in Japan get this visa, but it also applies to those involved in the entertainment industry that live here full-time. Models and actors also get this visa. Furthermore, it may apply to certain people in the entertainment industry aside from the performers themselves, such as those in management, promotion, post-production, etc.

Instructor Visa

This is the visa you would get as an ALT and there's not really much you can do with it other than that. Even to teach eikaiwa you'd need to switch over to a Specialist in Humanities Visa.

Investor / Business Manager Visa

This is the most difficult working visa to obtain and also the most risky. From the very beginning, it's important to understand that starting a business in Japan and applying for the Business Manager Visa are two separate things. Forming a company in Japan is not that cheap or easy to begin with, especially when compared to nearby jurisdictions like Hong Kong or Singapore. For those hoping to apply for a Business Manager Visa, there are even more hoops you need to jump through when forming your company so that you can be sure to get your visa approved later on.

The Legal Affairs Bureau which approves your company formation doesn't seem to care about your visa status, so it's entirely possible to start a company as a tourist or on another type of visa. However, if you intend to apply for a Business Manager Visa then you need to make sure you take all the proper steps from the very beginning. If your visa application gets denied then you'll be left with a company but no visa. That means you'll technically be working in Japan illegally.

Some of the steps you need to take in preparation for your visa application are writing up a proper business plan and hiring 2 full-time Japanese staff as well as an accountant. Last but not least, you need to invest a minimum of a whopping ¥5 million into your business! This is what makes the Business Manager Visa so risky. You could potentially follow all the steps and invest all of that money, but if the immigration bureau sees something wrong with your business plan then they still have the power to deny you a visa in the end.

If you really want to side-step this whole process while still being able to help form a company here, you need a Japanese person you can appoint as Representative

Director. According to June Advisors Group, "In the case where you're not eligible for the visa (status of residence) 'Business Manager' (lack of the amount of investment, etc.), the alternative options would be to find Japanese partners or other foreign investors, and apply for another type of visa status such as 'Specialist in Humanities / International Services' or 'Engineer.'"[24]

Even if your Japanese is excellent, I'd strongly recommend hiring a lawyer to guide you through the process.

Journalist Visa

Foreigners who are working for a foreign news organization in Japan get this visa. This includes work related to broadcasting, documentaries and also newspapers or magazines.

I've met a number of people doing journalism work in Japan on Specialist in Humanities Visas instead of Journalist Visas, although they were writing for magazines that wouldn't be categorized as news. If you want to work as a journalist, consult with your employer about which visa type you need.

Legal/Accounting Services Visa

This visa applies for those hoping to work as an attorney, scrivener or certified tax accountant. It's important to understand that you first must acquire certification in Japan and that in itself requires a lot of time studying here.

It's very difficult to work in these fields even if you're certified and have lots of experience in your home country.[25]

Medical Services Visa

This is for people who want to work as doctors, nurses, physicians, dentists, physical therapists, etc. Both the proper certification from your own country as well as the proper certification obtained in Japan are required. Japanese fluency is a must, and you will likely need to know all the kanji for all the relevant medical terms. Many applicants get rejected every year due to insufficient knowledge of Japanese medical terms and their kanji.

Professor Visa

Pretty self explanatory. This is the visa needed for foreigners teaching or working as assistants at universities in Japan.

Religious Activities

This is for people coming over to Japan to be something like a missionary or a priest. This is technically a work visa, so it's applicable for those who will be paid for whatever type of religious work they'll be doing. It may be possible to get special permission to do other types of work, such as part-time teaching. For those simply intending to study religion, a Cultural Activities Visa would probably be more appropriate.

Researcher Visa

This is a visa for people working at a research institute, or as researchers/investigators at a private or public organization, such as a university. There doesn't seem to be a lot of specific information about this category, unfortunately, and I've never met anyone living in Japan with this visa status.

Self-Sponsorship

"Self Sponsored" is not a visa category in itself, but refers to someone sponsoring themselves in a certain visa category as opposed to getting sponsored by an employer. It's usually possible in the Specialist in Humanities, Journalist, Skilled Labor or Engineer categories. The Investor/Business Manager Visa is also considered a type of "Self-sponsored" visa, although the requirements are much different. If you're not yet living in Japan, self-sponsorship will generally not be an option as your first visa here.

The key point is to be able to prove to immigration that your total income adds up to a certain amount, usually a minimum of ¥3 million per year. You need to prove this by showing all your work contracts and agreements. This could be a combination of contracts from part-time employers and agreements with private students or other clients.

Ashely Thompson of the *Japan Times* writes that

you should take "the documents with you to a nearby immigration office and apply for an 'extension of status' or 'change of status' to your visa. [Immigration lawyer Kyohei] Niitsu also suggests that 'you should declare that you will start your own freelance business to the tax office.' After that, you can get a special freelance certificate called the "*kojin jigyō no kaigyō todokede*."[26]

Skilled Labor Visa

This visa applies to specialized jobs such as civil engineering or a particular type of handicraft. It can also apply to jobs like animal training or piloting aircrafts. Depending on the type of work, the amount of experience required ranges from 3 - 10 years.[27]

A lot of foreigners in Japan want to work as a chef or a cook and a Skilled Labor Visa is required for these jobs as well. For chefs, the requirement is likely going to be 10 years experience and you'll also need a sponsor. You may even be required to provide the menus of restaurants where you've previously worked. Bear in mind that you might not be allowed to work in a restaurant specializing in a different cuisine from that of your home country, although it is very common to see Nepalese and Pakistanis working at Indian restaurants. Running your own restaurant would require the proper Business Manager Visa, not to mention a number of business licenses and health inspections.[28]

Specialist in Humanities / International Services

This is the visa you'll get as an eikaiwa teacher but it also applies to many other fields. Some notable examples include headhunting, graphic design, translation, marketing, PR, business coordination and even interior design. As you can tell, this is a very general visa category and there's a lot you can do with it. Usually anything involving the English language or something that requires a 'foreign perspective' can fit into this visa category.

While immigration won't ask any questions about the relation between your university degree and your job as an English teacher, they may do so for other Humanities/International Services jobs. You may be asked to provide evidence that you've studied something related to your job in college, or that you've acquired a certain amount of experience in that particular field before coming to Japan. Like many other things, this is determined on a case-by-case basis.

In some situations, when switching from one job to another that both fit under the broad "Specialist in Humanities" category, you may be required to fill out an "Application for Certificate of Authorized Employment." This simply confirms that your new job does in fact match your current visa status. You can take a look at the form here: http://www.immi-moj.go.jp/english/tetuduki/kanri/shyorui/10.html

Spousal Visa

If you're married to a Japanese citizen then you

can apply for this visa but it needs to be renewed every year. Aside from Permanent Residency, having Spousal Visa status gives you the most freedom. There are no restrictions on the type of work you can do which opens up so many opportunities that other foreigners do not have. This includes forming a new company without needing to apply for the Business Manager Visa, eliminating the requirement for a ¥5 million investment. Or you can do something simple like bartend, which none of the other visa categories allow foreigners to do.

After about 5 years of living in Japan on a Spousal Visa you can apply for Permanent Residency. If you become a Permanent Resident and then get a divorce, you're still allowed to remain in Japan. Getting a divorce without PR, however, would result in you being unable to renew your Spousal Visa again.

Student Visa

The Student Visa applies to any foreigner studying at a university or language school in Japan for over three months as well as high school foreign exchange students.

9

BEYOND TEACHING

Leaving the ESL bubble is not always easy. Most Japanese companies prefer to hire fresh college graduates they can train from scratch in return for unquestioning loyalty. Foreigners, meanwhile, are often required by the government to have 10 years of experience abroad before they can legally get most non-teaching jobs here. Since you likely won't be able to get hired while you're still the "blank slate" that traditional companies prefer, you really have to be able to offer something special that the average Japanese employee cannot.

It's best to get thinking about your next move early on if you already realize that teaching is not for you. Have a few hours free at your eikaiwa or ALT job? Why not take advantage of the time by studying code, design, or whatever it is you want to eventually do here, along with leveling up your Japanese skills?

If you know what type of company you want to join but are still working as a teacher, consider teaching business English lessons at companies in your desired industry. I've known a few people who were teaching English at a certain company, built up a good relationship with the staff and management and then eventually got hired by them as a regular employee.

If getting a job through a connection doesn't work out you could always go through a recruiting firm. There are also a lot of useful online resources for a wide variety of jobs in Japan. Checkout CareerCross.com, Daijob.com, or efinancialcareers.jp along with the usual Gaijinpot and Craigslist.

Other Career Paths

In the previous chapter I mentioned a number of different job options but mainly from a legal perspective. The following list focuses more on your chances of actually getting hired and earning a living in a given industry. The list not only includes industries that already have a lot of foreign workers but also jobs that are often asked about by newcomers to Japan. For a number of different reasons, not every job in this list is going to be a viable option for you. I simply hope to give you a general overview so that you can set realistic goals and expectations for yourself after taking your skills, language abilities and government requirements into consideration. If you have questions about a job that's not listed here, feel free to contact me and I'll hopefully be able to provide you with some more information.

Animation

A high percentage of foreigners coming to live in Japan have an interest in anime and some even dream of entering the industry themselves. It's important to understand, however, that many animators in Japan work under sweatshop-type conditions for salaries well below minimum wage. Young Japanese animators in their twenties are reported to earn salaries of less than $10,000 USD per year while working an average of 11 hours a day. The pay rises slightly with experience, but not by much. If you're an eikaiwa teacher that loves anime, consider the fact that you're currently earning around double the salary of many of the artists responsible for your favorite series. Of course, it should be pointed out that most people do it for the love of the art and not for the money.

If you still want to give it a shot, keep in mind that you'll be expected to already have a valid visa and Japanese language ability. Animator Henry Thurlow is one of a small handful of Westerners working at a major Japanese animation studio. If you're serious about becoming an animator here, I'd recommend looking him up and reading about some of his experiences in the industry.[29]

Artist or Musician

Unfortunately, the Japanese government does not have much interest in making Japan a place where foreign artists can come and earn a living. In the previous section I mentioned how difficult it can be to obtain an Artist Visa.

If that wasn't challenge enough, Japan is an especially tough place for artists and musicians to get by. This may be surprising to some considering Japan's thriving music and arts scene. It's actually pretty shocking how many well-known artists and musicians in Japan work normal full-time jobs to pay the bills.

Pay for musicians in particular is notably bad. I know a couple of foreign musicians living in Japan who are well-known enough to get booked around the world and get paid generously for their gigs in Europe and in the US. In Japan, however, they only get a small fraction of that pay. Instead of an artist visa they're here on some kind of teaching visa or a spousal visa if they're married.

If you're determined to live here as an artist, you may need to work as a teacher for a few years or more as you build up connections. If you find enough freelance work you could potentially self-sponsor yourself in the future or get hired by a company full-time. Or, you could set up your own business like a photography studio, for example. At the end of the day, Japan is an excellent place to get involved in art or music as a hobby but not so much as a profession.

Event Promotion

Some foreigners work as full-time event organizers in the rock, hip hop or electronic music scenes. If you lack a spousal visa, you'll likely need prior experience doing event production in your home country before being granted a visa here. The work itself can also be very stressful. You'll need to promote your events both online and by spreading physical flyers at clubs and music shops all throughout your city. Paying for airfare, hotels, local transport and dinner for the artists you're bringing over can make each event a big economic risk. With that said, the people who are successful at promotion end up making big money. (As I wrote above, it's typically the local musicians that are expected to work for dirt cheap while the promoters, venues and special guest artists rake in all the cash.) If promotion is something that interests you, you might want to be careful when choosing a style of music, as there is known to be some yakuza involvement in the more profitable scenes.

Graphic Design

Getting into the Japanese graphic design industry can be tough, although it does seem relatively open to foreigners. If you've worked as a designer in your home country, expect lower pay and longer hours than what you're used to (this is Japan, after all). Don't be surprised to be earning less than $20,000 USD a year when you're first starting out.

Graphic design in Japan is a highly competitive industry. Just by browsing through some magazines or event flyers, you can see that Japan has no shortage of skilled graphic artists. As a foreigner, you'll need to be able to bring something to the table that the average Japanese designer cannot, such as a certain style. In some cases, simply being bilingual could be enough.

You may be able to start out by getting an internship somewhere. As it would likely be unpaid, make sure you have enough cash saved up first. Or you might want to consider doing some freelance contract jobs here and there while you're still teaching. If you're lucky, you could eventually get a full-time job offer. Depending on your experience, degree and company that hires you, you may either need a Specialist in Humanities, Engineer or an Artist Visa.

Information Technology / Computer Engineer

Japan has a long way to go before achieving the tech startup culture of the United States or Europe, but there are still a lot of web and app development companies in the bigger cities that are actively seeking out foreigners.

If you're a programmer or developer, there are numerous IT job postings on sites like Gaijinpot or Craigslist. HTML, PHP, C++ and Javascript engineers appear to be in high demand. As smartphones have really taken off over the last several years, more and more app development companies are also looking for talented people.

If you have the right background and knowledge, IT is one of the most open industries for foreigners aside from teaching. The decent IT jobs pay from around ¥4 million - ¥7 million per year. Usually at least conversational Japanese ability is required.

I have no background in coding or programming whatsoever, but a few years ago I somehow managed to land an interview with a fairly well-known mobile app developer thanks to a referral from a friend. I was not surprised that they didn't give me an offer. I was more surprised by the fact that they even agreed to meet with me in the first place given my inexperience. Looking back, I think this is because on-the-job training is so common in Japan. I know some Japanese people with zero coding experience that got hired by app companies, received training and now develop apps full-time. On the one hand, you may not need as much experience as you might think because companies are so used to training people from scratch. But on the other hand, as a foreigner, you'll be competing with a lot of other Japanese who obviously speak the language fluently, so you should probably at least have some coding experience that the average person does not.

Journalist / Writer

There are quite a few English-language newspapers, magazines and web sites based in Japan. Even if you haven't had much published elsewhere but consider yourself to be a good writer, you may want to consider applying to some of these publications and see what happens. Maybe it won't become a full-time job but it could at least be a way to earn some extra cash on the side. Just by looking on Craigslist you can find a lot of people looking for writers, especially Japan-related travel writers. Searching through the postings, I see some people offering no pay at all, others offering around ¥2,000 per article, and then even one position for ¥5,000 an hour!

To write full time you'll need a visa. If you're a freelance writer then immigration will probably want you to have some recognizable web sites or magazines listed on your resume. You may also want to consider joining the

Foreign Correspondent's Club.

Photographer

There are a number of opportunities to become a photographer in Japan. Just like anywhere else, wedding photographers are always in demand. Whenever I go to a music event I see an event photographer hired by the organizers and sometimes it's a foreigner. Given the vacation rental property boom going on in Japan right now, there are even a number of foreigners employed by Airbnb and similar companies to take interior shots of people's properties. If you can't find steady employment as a photographer, you could always start your own company. That's much easier said than done but it's not impossible.

Depending on the type of photography you're doing, different types of visas may be required. If you're employed by a newspaper, for example, you could get a Journalist Visa. If you're a freelance photographer with enough experience for immigration to be happy, you would probably get an Artist Visa.

I think most foreign photographers in Japan are probably just doing it on the side in addition to their main job. If you really have the passion and drive to become a full-time photographer then it's best to make the right connections early on and start building up your portfolio.

Military

There are a number of U.S. citizens stationed at military bases throughout Japan. Some people who get sent here by chance end up falling in love with the country and staying permanently. But it would be silly to recommend joining the military just for the possibility of getting to live in Japan. Also be aware that military personnel don't always have the best reputations in the towns where they're stationed, especially in Okinawa, although that's not necessarily the case everywhere.

Modeling / TV Personality / Movie Extra

Many foreigners in Japan do a little bit of modeling, even if they never would've considered pursuing it back home. Outside of major train stations you might encounter scouts looking for foreign models. They may also be looking for people to be an extra in a TV show or movie or appear on a Japanese variety show. If you want to actively pursue modeling or TV work and not just wait to get scouted, try getting head shots and portraits taken by a professional photographer in different settings before promoting yourself.

Aspiring models or actors may also want to use an agency. By using an agent you'll have a higher chance of getting auditions but the agent will in turn take a significant percentage of your pay. Remember that an agent is not your employer and therefore cannot sponsor you for a visa. You'll either have to find steady employment from a single company or get enough work every month to convince immigration to grant you a freelance or self-sponsored visa.[30]

I've never done any modeling but from what I hear, a lot of time can be wasted spending an entire day at an audition or casting call for a part you don't end up getting.

That can be tough for a full-time worker with only 2 days off per week. On the other hand, the jobs that you do land can pay generously. Some people eventually quit their teaching jobs to focus on attending more auditions and casting calls. If things work out, they can even earn significantly more than they did as a teacher.

An advertising agency may have a very specific look in mind when searching for someone to promote their product. You never know, you might just end up in the right place at the right time. Naturally, appearing in a major ad or commercial will suddenly open up the doors for more and more opportunities.

Music Teacher

If you're a skilled musician and have some experience giving lessons in your home country, it may be possible to get a job teaching music in Japan. In the bigger cities, there are bilingual music schools and even some that operate predominantly in English, so Japanese ability may not even be a requirement. The schools will likely want you to have at least attended a well-known music college such as Berklee College of Music.

Nurse / Doctor

Japan does allow some foreign nurses, most of whom are women from the Philippines, Indonesia, China and other Asian countries. There's some controversy over the issue because while many of these nurses are highly qualified, experienced, and even fluent in Japanese, they must pass the Japanese nursing exam which is full of complex kanji. Due to the difficulty of the exam, only about 10% of Indonesian and Filipino applicants succeed in becoming nurses here. This is in spite of Japan's rapidly aging population and the ever growing demand for caretakers and medical workers.

If you want to become a nurse in Japan, you'll either need to get certified in your own country and then pass the notoriously difficult nursing exam here, or start studying from scratch in Japan. This would also require Japanese and kanji fluency, of course. Male nurses are pretty much unheard of in Japan but that may be slowly changing.

The process to become a doctor is similar. Either you must first obtain a license elsewhere and then pass the test in Japan, or you need to attend a Japanese medical school. Again, extremely proficient Japanese language ability will be required in either case, even well beyond the JLPT N1 level. If you do obtain this level of proficiency, your bilingual skills could be a great advantage to you, as English-speaking doctors in Japan are still pretty hard to come by.

Proofreader

To get a proofreading job you'll need a valid degree and extensive knowledge of a particular field, such as medicine, biology or finance. It's also best if you have good Japanese ability, as sometimes you'll need to consult the original writing if you can't make sense of the English. However, even with the proper skills and knowledge of a specific niche, you need to be registered with an agency and take their exam before they'll help you find work. Since there's also not a lot of demand for English proofreaders at the moment, you may have difficulty finding a full-time job. If you're fluent in another language besides English than you might have a better chance.[31]

Real Estate Agent

Due to the difficult process of renting an apartment in Japan, there are an increasing number of services popping up to help foreigners find a place to live. Many of these are staffed by foreigners themselves. To work at a real estate agent you are going to need excellent Japanese skills in order to communicate with landlords and explain contracts to your clients. You'll also need extensive knowledge of the apartment rental process. There isn't much information out there on what type of visa these jobs require, but if your job involves English communication, a Humanities visa would likely be appropriate. To actually start your own real estate business you'd need a special license obtained by passing an exam which, of course, is going to be all in Japanese.

Tour Guide

Becoming a tour guide as a foreigner is not as easy as you might think. This is yet another profession that requires passing a test to obtain a special license, and (surprise!) the test is only in Japanese. That means that even if you want to work with non-Japanese tourists who do not speak the local language, you still need to have near native-level Japanese ability to pass the exam. You'll also be required to know a lot about Japanese history as a whole, no matter how knowledgable you are about the specific city or region you want to work in.

It probably wouldn't be difficult to advertise and arrange small, informal tours via Craigslist. I wouldn't recommend this, however, as getting caught without a license could result in a ¥500,000 fine!

Translator / Interpreter

If your Japanese skills are JLPT N1 level or even better, being a translator is a career path you might consider. Keep in mind that simply having amazing Japanese skills is not enough. You need to be very knowledgeable about the topic that you're translating from the original Japanese. If not, you at least need to do extensive research on it before and during each job. Furthermore, you have to be a very good writer in English or in your other native language. If you're translating fiction, you should already have lots of prior experience reading Japanese novels and have the ability to get a sense of an author's voice.

Most translators are freelancers who do contract jobs and have strict deadlines to adhere to. Unfortunately, the pay for most translation work in Japan isn't great. I've met a number of half-Japanese and *nikkei* who were raised fully bilingual and who do some translation work on the side, but most tell me it doesn't pay enough to be worth focusing on full-time. I've also met some foreigners who became qualified translators after lots of hard work and study. They've also said that it's not much more than a side gig. However, I'm not sure if any of these people were experts in one particular field. You might have a chance of getting better paying contract work or even full-time work if you have a specialization in a certain industry.

Interpretation work generally pays better but jobs can be harder to get. Depending on your connections, you might be able to get some part-time interpreting work and see where it goes from there. I've done interpreting any number of times for foreign musicians touring Japan and while the pay wasn't great in my case, it was at least pretty fun. I've heard that the pay is excellent for interpreters working with foreign pro baseball players, so if you have a special interest in sports that's something you may want to look into.

Video Game Industry

Considering the amount of people around the world who first got acquainted with Japanese culture through video games, it's only natural that a lot of foreigners dream of entering the local gaming industry. The good news is that there are plenty of opportunities for foreigners, but you first have to convince a company to hire you over a local. Not only do you need the relevant technical skills but the more Japanese you know the better. If you're involved in the development process, expect to be working extremely long hours, rarely returning home before the last train of the night.

Even without any programming, artistic or Japanese language skills, there are still some opportunities for proofreading translations of unfinished games. These jobs are typically very low paying and you can only get work per project and not full-time. If you really want to get involved in the industry then it could still be a good way to establish some connections, potentially enabling you to move on to something more secure in the future.

Work for Yourself / Entrepreneur

As mentioned in the previous section, the Investor/Business Manager Visa is one of the most expensive and riskiest visas to get. However, if you've read this far already then I'm sure you realize that getting a job in Japan as a foreigner is not easy. And not only that, but even if you do get into your industry of choice, you have to deal with the same bullshit that the average Japanese worker has to deal with - long hours, substandard pay, strict office hierarchy, lack of free time, lack of flexibility and did I mention the extremely long hours? Starting your own business is not simple or cheap, but it's probably the best choice if you're determined to live in Japan long-term and want as much freedom, prosperity and personal fulfillment as possible.

Foreign entrepreneurs in Japan have an advantage because the Japanese are generally quite risk averse. Even if there's an untapped market that many people openly acknowledge has potential, the Japanese will typically wait until someone else tries it first. If it's proven to be successful, only then will they jump on the bandwagon and set up a similar company. As a foreigner, you have the chance to be an innovator and start new businesses that local entrepreneurs are reluctant to attempt. That being said, not everyone has to be an innovator and plenty of people around the world do very well with tried and true business models. With that in mind, you could look into taking an idea from a successful Japanese company and adapting it for the English-speaking market.

There is so much you need to consider when starting a business in Japan. Are your customers going to be mostly Japanese, foreign residents or short-term tourists? Are you going to sell your product or service to other businesses or directly to customers? A lot of this will determine how well you need to familiarize yourself with Japanese business customs and how good your language skills need to be. There are a number of services and lawyers you can hire to give you the proper advice and help you set up your company. If your language ability is less than perfect, and even if it is perfect, hiring someone for help is a smart choice.

Conclusion

This is by no means a complete list of all the jobs that foreigners can do here, but hopefully you now have an idea of what it takes to get started on other career paths. This list has hopefully encouraged you but it's also possibly scared you away from trying to leave the ESL industry. That's understandable, as it's obvious that there are a lot of deliberate barriers in place to prevent foreigners from finding non-teaching jobs. But even with those obstacles in your path, it all really comes down to what your dream is and how badly you want to live here.

If you just can't stand teaching anymore yet still don't feel you have the skills or experience to enter one of the above-mentioned industries, there's still one other job in Japan that's very easy for foreigners to get...

Headhunting

For whatever reason, headhunting is one of the easiest industries for foreigners in Japan to enter. While there's all sorts of red tape preventing *gaijin* from getting most non-teaching jobs, the Japanese government is totally fine with foreigners working as headhunters, even with zero experience in the field. The visa required for headhunting is the same Specialist in Humanities Visa that eikaiwa teachers get, making the transition from teaching an easy one. Most recruiting companies don't expect you to have any special degree or background either, but they do often prefer that you have some prior experience living in Japan.

* * *

Note: To be clear, I am not talking about using a recruiting firm to help you find a job. I'm talking about working as a recruiter yourself. Sure, feel free to contact a recruiting firm to help you with your job search, but if all you have is a basic liberal arts degree and are not fully bilingual, don't expect much from them. They won't charge you any money and it's not a scam, but after reading what most recruiters in Japan actually do, you'll have an idea of what to expect as a candidate.

* * *

There are many recruiting firms in Tokyo that consist of mostly foreign staff. A lot of these firms focus on finding suitable candidates for foreign companies (*gaishikei*) which have branches here. There are thousands of recruiters in Tokyo alone which may sound odd considering how uncommon it is in Japan for people to switch jobs mid-career. Evidently, there are still enough Japanese workers willing to change jobs to keep all these recruiting firms in business.

The companies your employer will have as clients are searching for suitable candidates for specific positions. These positions often have very particular requirements and the clients are typically extremely selective. Most companies are not interested in unemployed people or even in those actively trying to switch jobs. They often feel that the best people are those that are already happily employed and not even thinking about a change. As a headhunter, it's your job to find these candidates (preferably from one of your client's main competitors) and pitch them the new position. If they're interested, you then submit their resume to your client. It can be a lot of work getting even that far, and then the challenge is only beginning.

Next you have to talk up the candidate to your client. If they're not interested, you just have to keep scouting candidates and submitting more resumes. Meanwhile, there may be several other recruiting firms working on the same position for your client and they'll often beat you to the punch. It's not uncommon for weeks or months of scouting to go down the drain this way.

If you do make a successful placement, the company you work for will receive a percentage (usually 30 - 35%) of the placed candidate's new yearly salary. Out of that money, you or your team will receive a percentage as commission. Depending on the company, the recruiter who placed the candidate may take all the bonus money for him or herself or they may divide it amongst their team. The higher the successfully placed candidate's new salary, of course, the higher the commission. This new salary is naturally going to be higher than the old one, otherwise there'd be no point in changing jobs. Unless, of course, the candidate's former employer was involved in some kind of scandal. Corporate scandals are quite common here and are also the ideal time for headhunters to pounce.

How do you find suitable candidates in the first place? It depends on the recruiting firm, but when you first start out at the job you'll probably have to make lots and lots of cold calls. If you're uncomfortable with lying or deceiving people in any way then this is not the job for you. People usually decide very quickly if this is something they can handle. Hence, some companies will even make the interviewee try out some cold calls as a test. Even after making it through the interview stage, people quitting on their first or second day is not at all uncommon.

When you first start the job you'll be assigned to a certain industry. Some smaller recruiting firms specialize entirely in one area while larger firms will serve clients in all kinds of industries like IT, finance, industrial and gaming. Before you pick up the phone you'll first need to do some online research about Japanese companies in the industry you've been assigned to. You then call up a company and tell the receptionist how you're trying to get in touch with a sales rep/marketing manager/engineer you recently met at a trade show. The problem is, however, you've forgotten his name! If only she would kindly go through some of the names of people in that department, you'd surely remember who it was! If the call goes as planned, she'll read off several names as you have a pen and paper handy, writing down everything she says. As a rule, none of the names she gives you are ever going to be correct. End the call by saying you'll have another look for the misplaced business card and call again later. Does this sound awkward or uncomfortable to you at all? Well you better get used to it, because in the beginning that's pretty much all you'll be doing every day for weeks or even months.

Several days after getting a set of names from a certain company, you then choose one of those names from your list at random and call back that same company. The reason you have to wait several days is so that by now the receptionist has hopefully forgotten your voice. You now ask for the random name you've chosen from your list, and when you get him (or occasionally her) on the phone, your new mission is to set up a face-to-face meeting with this mystery person. You explain how he was "highly recommended" by a colleague whose name you cannot mention. You tell him that you have information about an excellent new position and it would be great if the two of you could meet in person to discuss the details.

Only about 1 in every 10 or so of these calls will ever be successful. If the call goes well then you'll meet the guy, either at your office or somewhere neutral like a coffee shop, and interview him about his skills and background. If he's relevant to the job you're scouting for, pitch him the position and promise that you can arrange to get him a higher salary than what he's currently making. Since the whole cold-calling thing is nothing but a random numbers game, most of the time the people you meet won't be suitable at all for what you're scouting for. Even if their skills and background are relevant, the guy could be a fresh college grad or even a 67-year-old man. You still have to pretend he was "recommended" and that you called him on purpose, making the whole situation even more awkward. Instead of pitching him the position, just mumble something about how you'll "get in touch when we have something for you."

Not every company makes you cold call to collect names. Some have several staff members whose job it is to cold call for you. The recruiters can then spend more time searching through the company database or LinkedIn for suitable candidates. While LinkedIn is a very valuable tool, there are still lots of workers in Japan who aren't on it which is why cold calling still exists. Also, sometimes you really will get referrals from other candidates that you meet, in which case the whole "I've heard a lot about you" line won't actually be a lie.

If the process I've just described wasn't uncomfortable, tedious and soul-crushing enough, recruiters are under enormous stress and pressure from their bosses and managers to make the company money. If you're not placing candidates you're essentially a waste of the company's time and resources. Upper management won't hesitate to remind employees of this fact. People often get fired on the spot to set an example. Many more recruiters leave voluntarily, while the more successful ones are often scouted themselves by rival headhunting firms.

If the pressure and threats from management weren't enough, there's also the fact that you can never really trust the people you work with. A lot of drama happens when one recruiter scouts candidates from their coworker's client. If this client company finds out that the same recruiting firm they've been cooperating with has actually been trying to steal their own people behind their backs, all deals are off and your employer will likely end up on a blacklist. Some major big money deals can suddenly get called off this way. Office confrontations between two coworkers that actually escalate into fistfights are not unheard of!

On the other hand, it's important to point out that not every single headhunter is a greedy, sleazy backstabber. There are a lot of really good, friendly and down-to-earth people working in the industry, too. It's just not always obvious who people really are in the beginning. If you've ever seen the movie *The Wolf of Wall Street*, the office atmosphere is pretty similar to that, minus the drugs and hookers. Unsurprisingly, a lot of crazy eccentric types flock to this industry. They can at least provide you with some mild entertainment and funny memories if you don't end up coming out of it rich.

Why Be a Headhunter?

After reading all of this, you're probably wondering why anyone in their right mind would want to become a headhunter in Japan. The number one reason is simple:

money. Headhunting is one of the only (legal) jobs in which someone with a generic liberal arts degree from an average university can come and start earning six figures within a couple of years. No special skills are required other than being very persistent and somewhat ruthless. Some people who are excellent at it can even become millionaires.

If you work as a headhunter in Japan you'll notice how many people have come straight from teaching. As you're already aware, the standard teaching salary is around ¥250,000 and hardly ever increases. The thought of potentially earning double or triple or even several times more than that is naturally going to be very appealing to many people. Some teachers end up starting families in Japan and feel they have no other option if they want to adequately support their children. Others become recruiters in order to support a sick relative. And then there's the majority that just want to get rich, and I don't think there's anything inherently wrong with that.

Money aside, another reason why so many teachers switch over to recruiting reveals more about the ESL industry itself than it does about headhunting. From the perspective of an eikaiwa teacher, being a recruiter actually feels somewhat like a *real* job. Most teachers don't get taken seriously by their bosses, have no opportunities for a promotion and job security is incredibly shaky. As unpleasant as headhunting may be, recruiters actually receive tangible benefits for their hard work in the form of bonuses. Furthermore, their performance, whether good or bad, is immediately recognized by the company. A common complaint from teachers in Japan is that they almost never receive any positive feedback from their bosses, leading to low morale and a lack of motivation in the long run.

If you've read all this and still want to give headhunting a shot then by all means go for it. To be clear, you will be receiving a base salary, sometimes even slightly higher than a teacher's salary. Don't think your pay will be completely dependent on bonuses. In fact, many headhunters work for a year or more before ever making a placement. Ideally, if you make a placement you get a bonus, but it's not really that simple in reality. Everyone has their own "account" with their employer and each month that you receive your base salary, that amount gets subtracted from this account. For example, if it's your 3rd month without a placement (after an initial grace period is over) you're now around ¥750,000 in the red. If you then make your first placement that's on the small to medium side, for example, you probably won't receive any bonus money. That would just bring you up to being ¥300,000 or so in the red.

Understand that you'll never actually be in debt to the company and they will always keep paying you your base salary. The amount you are in the red, however, is very clear evidence of how much money the company's wasted on keeping you employed. You'll be reminded of where you stand constantly.

As I mentioned earlier, the successful recruiters do really become quite wealthy, but most people just fizzle out before they get anywhere. And the ones who do make it to the top continually have to work 11-12 hours a day just to stay there. If you're looking for personal fulfillment, you'd actually be better off as an English teacher. But if you find yourself in a desperate situation or just dream of getting rich quickly, succeeding as a headhunter in Japan is one possible way to earn lots of cash in a short amount of time.

10

RENTING AN APARTMENT

Finding a good apartment is difficult anywhere in the world, but the whole process in Japan can be especially confusing and expensive. There are also a number of obstacles you'll encounter as a foreigner that the average Japanese citizen doesn't have to deal with. But if you're desperate to get out of your cramped share house or company housing and finally get some peace and privacy, making the effort to move into your own place will be worth it in the end. This chapter will help guide you through the process.

Fees and Useful Terms

Renting in Japan involves paying a lot more upfront fees than would be normal, or even legal, in many other countries. The one positive side to renting an apartment here is that you're usually not bound to live in a single place for a fixed period of time. While you will be required to give your landlord notice (in most cases a month) before moving out, there shouldn't be any penalty for leaving even a couple months into your lease. That's likely the reason for there being so many upfront fees.

Below is a list of all the different fees that you'll generally have to pay up front:

Shikikin (敷金)

This just means deposit money, and you will usually have to pay one month's rent of *shikikin* up front. Some landlords may even request double for nicer places. *No big deal*, you may be thinking, *I'll just get all of it back when I move out, right?* Sorry, but not really, no. Many rental agreements contain small print which guarantees a large chunk of your deposit staying with the landlord. For example, your contract may state that most of your *shikikin* can be used to clean and refurbish the apartment for the tenants after you, regardless of how well you took care of the place. Even if you just live in an apartment for a month and then suddenly need to leave, it's somewhat rare to get all of your deposit money back. If you're lucky, you'll get at least some of it, but it's not unheard of to get nothing at all.

Reikin (礼金)

Reikin is gift money. Gift money for whom? The landlord. Why? For the "privilege" of being allowed to live in their apartment, of course! Yes, you read that right. Even if you end up in a tiny apartment not much bigger than a cardboard box, with walls so thin you can hear your neighbors snore, you still need to give your landlord a gift for this rare opportunity. Usually this is one month's rent, but for nicer places it can be up to two.

On sites like Suumo it's possible to search for apartments with no *reikin*. This will greatly reduce the search results but there are some surprisingly nice places out there that don't require it. Hopefully the market pushes things more and more in that direction from now on.

Hoshounin (保証人)

This refers to a guarantor, or someone who will be legally responsible if you suddenly bail and skip out on the rent. Japanese people need guarantors too, and often use a sibling, parent or a close friend. No matter how many close Japanese friends you have, however, single foreigners are often not allowed to use anything other than a *hoshougaisha*, or guarantor company. The real estate agent or building management company will usually set you up with one, so it's normally not necessary to find one on your own. You'll need to pay this company half a month's rent when you first move in and then ¥10,000 per year for as long as you remain there.

Something I still don't quite understand is that even though you cannot use a Japanese friend or resident as a guarantor, you're still often required to put someone's info down in case of an emergency. I don't plan to skip out on my rent anytime soon, but if I did, I'm not sure how much responsibility, if any, would fall on my "emergency contact" instead of my guarantor company.

Real Estate Agent Fee

Another fee you'll have to shell out is the fee for the real estate agent. This is also usually a month's rent. Even if you're aware that a particular apartment is vacant, you'll still be required to use a real estate agent and pay them for the "introduction." It's almost unheard of to negotiate with the landlord directly unless it's an acquaintance of yours. This is just one of many examples in Japan of being forced to pay a middle man even when you don't need one.

Some real estate agents have campaigns where you only have to pay them 50%. Others, in small print somewhere, may actually expect more than one month's rent. If you don't like dealing with a particular real estate agency but are keen on a certain apartment, you can usually just take the apartment info to another agency who would be happy to "introduce" you all over again.

Insurance

When you move you'll have to pay for things like fire, flood or natural disaster insurance. Your real estate agent will explain all of this to you. When it's time to renew your contract after two years, you'll have to pay these fees again.

Japanese Apartment Types

Apaato (Apartment) *and Manshon* (Mansion)

Japan uses many English loan words, often in a different context from their original English meaning. *Manshon* is one of these terms. It just refers to an apartment, yet one that's considered nicer than a regular *apaato*. *Apaato's* are generally older with very thin walls, while *manshon*'s are more modern and often made of concrete. When you visit a real estate agent you'll often be asked which of the two you prefer. There are many places that blur the lines between the two, however.

1K, 2DK, 2LDK, etc.

Aside from *apaato* and *manshon*, there are a number of other terms, or more accurately, codes, that you'll notice when looking at a Japanese apartment listing. You'll always see letters like R, D, L or K with a number attached.

The most basic type of apartment you can find is a 1R which is just a single room studio apartment. A 1R apartment is usually small but some 1R places can be quite spacious. Next is the 1K, which is like a 1R but with a separate kitchen. A 1R apartment will always have a kitchen but it's usually nothing more than a small sink with a single stove next to it.

Next there are multiple room types like the 1DK, 1LDK, 2DK, 2LDK, etc. 'D' stands for dining room while 'L' stands for living room, or really just any room that's neither a bedroom or a kitchen. The numbers at the beginning simply refer to the number of bedrooms. Therefore, a 2LDK has 2 bedrooms, a living room and a separate dining room and kitchen. Small families usually live in a 2 or 3LDK. If you're looking for a budget apartment in the central part of a big city, you're not going to want to consider much more than a 1R or a 1K. Obviously, the further out in the countryside you go, the more affordable something like a 1LDK or a 2DK becomes.

Be sure to check the actual size of the apartment in square meters. You might come across a 1LDK apartment that's divided up into rooms so tiny that there's not even enough space for a double bed. In that case you'd be better off with a 1R of the same size. I actually prefer 1R or 1K apartments myself because they give you a lot more freedom when it comes to the layout and interior design.

Jou

Aside from square meters, the size of Japanese apartments or rooms are also measured by tatami mats. That doesn't necessarily mean that the room has actual tatami. It's just a measurement of how many mats could fit. For a basic cheap studio apartment in Tokyo, a total floor space of around 6 - 10 *jou* is typical.

The Process

If you haven't been scared off yet by the thought of

all those upfront fees, here's how you actually hunt for an apartment. I'm going to be using Tokyo as an example, but the same basic process would apply in any city.

You can find a lot of apartment listings simply by searching online. As far as Japanese real estate sites go, I prefer using Suumo.jp and Chintai.net. There are some English search engines out there as well, notably the "Apartments" section of Gaijinpot, although the prices appear to be higher than on Suumo. Just judging from my own knowledge and experience with rental prices in certain neighborhoods of Tokyo, it seems like you'll be paying a few more *man* per month in rent by using the English language sites. If you want to have a go at using a Japanese site, try installing the rikaikun/rikaichan plugins for your browser which automatically translate Japanese words that you hover over with your mouse.

All of these web sites have handy search functions that let you narrow down your search to a certain area, such as Shinjuku-ku, Shibuya-ku or Musashino-shi. You can also search by train lines and specific stations. You can even set parameters for size and rent, and other specific things like whether or not you require a Japanese-style bathroom. Want to live no more than a 7 minute walk from Ikebukuro station in a 30 square meter apartment, or maybe anywhere in Shibuya-ku for under ¥80,000 a month? You should be able to find just what you're looking for. As mentioned earlier, there's also the option to search for apartments with no *reikin* or *shikikin* but doing so will greatly limit your results.

Once you find a place that catches your eye there will be information and a telephone number for a particular real estate agency somewhere on the screen. Sometimes the exact same listing will be uploaded to these sites multiple times, each one by a different agency. Understand in advance that some agencies will intentionally leave attractive but already occupied listings on the site in hopes of getting more inquiries. Others may just be lazy and forget to take the listings down. Don't be surprised if the place you had your eye on is already occupied.

Ideally, assuming the apartment is still available, you just call up the agency and meet the agent in front of the building at a scheduled time. Then they'll just show you around the apartment and answer your questions. This is how it should, and sometimes does actually work if you're lucky. What happens more often, however, is that the agency you call up will insist that you come to their office first to fill out some basic forms. Only after that will they accompany you to the apartment.

Once you arrive at the office, it's common for them to "suddenly discover" that the apartment is no longer available. "No problem," they'll tell you. "There are plenty of very similar apartments that we can show you. Just have a seat." From personal experience, the other apartments they show you often won't meet your criteria and you'll likely end up wasting an entire afternoon. You just have to continue calling up different agencies and keep trying.

Ignoring the online search function altogether, you could always just visit a real estate agent from the get-go and tell them what you have in mind. The agent will typically print out 10 or so sheets of paper with info for a certain apartment on each one, and then you'll narrow it down to 3 or 4 that you want to see in person that day. This is also very hit-or-miss, but I have been shown some great apartments this way. The whole process is just one big numbers game.

Most Japanese real estate agencies don't have any English speaking staff, so it's best if you speak Japanese already or can go with someone who does. If this entire process sounds very daunting to handle in Japanese, I recommend just visiting a specialized English-language real estate agent from the get-go. For those based in Tokyo, some companies you might want to check out are Flat (flat-japan.com) and Housing Japan (housingjapan.com). If you're located elsewhere, a basic online search should help you find what you're looking for.

Discrimination

One thing the real estate agent will need to confirm over the phone with the landlord is whether or not foreigners are allowed to live there. Keep in mind that there are no anti-discrimination laws in Japan and landlords don't need to give any reason for not allowing foreigners. Some landlords are only fine with certain nationalities or races, so don't be shocked to hear the agent discussing this over the phone right in front of you. Some landlords are fine with any foreigner but only as long as they can speak conversational Japanese.

When apartment hunting in Japan, it's unfortunately quite normal to get rejected many times simply because you're not Japanese. I've even been close to signing a rental agreement for a place that supposedly allowed foreigners when the landlord suddenly backed out at the last minute. While he was ok with foreigners, he'd just talked to his racist wife who said she didn't want any! When foreigners are allowed, it's not uncommon to see something like "Pets and foreigners OK" advertised on the information sheet. Welcome to 21st century Japan!

Cost of Rent

Japanese cities are known around the world for their high cost of living. Compared to other major cities like New York, San Francisco or London, however, rent is surprisingly affordable in Japan, provided you can handle living in such a tight space.

In central Shibuya, Tokyo, for example, which is more or less Tokyo's equivalent to Times Square, it's possible to find an apartment in the ¥80,000 - ¥100,000 a month range. Sure, that's not cheap for someone just getting started in the country and the apartment itself will be pretty shabby and tiny, but it's much more affordable than most people would assume. Rent in central Shinjuku, roughly Tokyo's equivalent to Midtown Manhattan, would cost about the same. With that in mind, you can find some really affordable apartments just a few stops away from Tokyo's busiest stations.

Of course, a lot depends on whether you'll be living alone or with a friend or partner. One thing I like about Japan is how affordable it is to live alone. You don't need to live with 2 or 3 other roommates just to afford rent like in other parts of the world. In fact, most budget apartments are built with a single occupant in mind. If you're looking to live with someone, sharing a single 1R apartment would be tough so I'd go for at least a 1LDK, or maybe even a small house.

Osaka and Kyoto have much cheaper rent compared to Tokyo, which is a major plus considering how teaching salaries are about the same. Obviously, the further you go out in the countryside the cheaper everything gets. It's no wonder why JET's are able to save so much money.

Necessary Documents

Now that you've finally found your dream apartment you'll need to fill out an application form. The real estate agent will forward this on to the landlord or management company. Other things you'll need to provide are documentation to prove you have stable income. You'll need to show them a couple of recent pay slips to prove this and you may also be asked to print out a bank statement. They will also request a copy of your Residence Card and possibly even passport.

Be aware that your guarantor company will at some point call your place of employment to confirm you really work there. They'll usually just call up and ask the secretary if you're there that day without explaining why they're calling. It's normal and not a big deal, so don't be surprised if you find out that they've called. With that said, be totally honest with them about where you work.

Buying Furniture

Most apartments in Japan are unfurnished which means you'll need to spend even *more* money on buying furniture. The Japanese even have a term called *hikkoshi-bimbou* which means being "broke from moving."

Here are some options I recommend when furnishing your new place:

IKEA

If you've ever been to an IKEA anywhere in the world then you know exactly what to expect. The furniture and most of the other products will be the same as what you can get back home. At the time of writing, IKEA in Japan still doesn't allow you to order online. If you don't have a driver's license or car then you'll have to go to the store yourself, choose your items and get them delivered at a later date. Considering how far IKEA is from most city centers, the whole process can be a real hassle.

Nitori

This is a budget furniture chain found throughout the country. The types of goods and their prices are pretty similar to what you'd find at IKEA, but the designs are unique to Japan. Nitori allows you to order online but the web site is in Japanese only. When visiting any store, they'll only have the smaller items available for purchase right then and there and you'll need to schedule a delivery for most furniture.

Shopping at Nitori can be frustrating because they always seem to have some kind of stock issue. Not only will many of the items you want not be there at the actual store, they'll often need to be put on back order as well. It's not uncommon to have to wait over 2 or 3 weeks before the product can be delivered to your new place.

Mujirushi

This is a popular chain that also has some stores abroad. The furniture and other goods are minimalistic and stylish but they also come with a price. I like Mujirushi for their beds. While not the cheapest option out there, they're still relatively affordable and are very comfortable. They also sell good pillows for only ¥1,200 each.

Local recycle shop

There are lots of recycle shops throughout Japan. Some sell all kinds of furniture while others might only sell appliances like refrigerators and washing machines. If you live relatively close by to one and spend over a certain amount of money, many shops will deliver the items for you that day or the next for free.

Craigslist / JMTY

The local Craigslist pages for Japan are not nearly

as active as in other countries but they're still worth a look. Throwing away large items is a major pain in Japan so many foreigners give away their unwanted furniture or appliances for free or very cheap. The catch is that the buyer will have to go pick it up him or herself and pay for a car rental.

A Japanese site called JMTY has also recently become popular as a way for people to get rid of their unwanted stuff. Like with Craigslist, you'll need your own vehicle but a lot of the stuff is free. The site is all in Japanese but you can check it out at jmty.jp.

Rakuten, Nissen and Amazon.jp

These are all popular online stores that sell a wide variety of furniture items. Since it's the internet, you won't be able to see the items in person and the pictures can be deceptive. I bought a cheap bed once from Nissen that started to cave in less than a year after I bought it. Getting rid of it and buying a new bed was not an easy or cheap process, as I'll explain shortly. Still, if you're on a tight budget and you're not picky, you might want to give one of these sites a try. Amazon is great for smaller stuff like rugs or lamps.

Who You Will Deal With

Many tenants in Japan never deal with their landlords directly or even ever meet them. Instead you'll probably be dealing with a management company (*kanrigaisha*). When you have problems in your apartment, such as a clogged drain or a broken air con remote, you can call up your management company to have them come fix it for free. Your total rent will include a "management fee" you pay every month for these services.

I've had good experiences overall with the management companies in control of the places I've lived. One time my air conditioner remote stopped working and since it was an older model, they just installed an entire brand new air con unit for no charge! But I do know people that have gotten stuck with neglectful companies that kept making excuses to not show up.

While many people never even meet their landlord, you may find yourself living in the same building as your landlord and you might be seeing them every day. When signing your rental contract it's best to confirm exactly who it is you're supposed to contact in case of any problems.

Garbage Disposal

Japan is very strict when it comes to garbage disposal and the system is overwhelmingly complicated. Depending on where you live, there will be certain days for disposing different types of garbage. If you live in a larger building, you may have access to a disposal area where you can throw things out at any time or day, assuming it's been separated properly. Apartment buildings (or *manshons*) often have a doorman or caretaker who won't hesitate to tell you if you've been putting things out incorrectly. If you're not lucky enough to have access to one of these disposal areas then you have no choice but to let stuff pile up in your apartment as garbage day approaches.

The number one rule with trash disposal here is that cans and bottles can never be thrown out with the regular trash. Garbage must be disposed of in transparent bags so if you have a can or bottle in there and the garbage collectors notice, they'll just leave your entire bag there with a warning note! Furthermore, when throwing out bottles, you're expected to remove both the cap and the plastic labelling. Depending on where you live, people may or may not actually follow this rule.

Your ward or city office can provide you with a detailed but confusing guide on which trash can be thrown out on which days. Regular trash is normally picked up twice a week, while there's often only one day a week to get rid of your bottles/cans, cardboard and plastics. Most cities don't care about styrofoam and plastic containers being included in the regular burnable trash, while other districts are very strict and will send you a warning notice if you mess up.

Why is this all so strict? After years of living here it still remains a mystery to me. Are all these disposal rules there because of the limited space in the country? Or is it just a result of Japan's tendency to unnecessarily overcomplicate simple things? Probably a combination of the two.

Furniture Disposal

If you have any furniture to get rid of, you'll need to call your city office and arrange for them to pick it up. This is called *sodaigomi*. There is typically only one *sodaigomi* day a week for any given area. In densely populated areas, the *sodaigomi* reservations can be booked up for weeks or over a month in advance. If you're replacing an older piece of furniture with something new, be sure to have your disposal day reserved and confirmed before ordering new stuff. Oh, and don't forget - even though you're already paying a bunch of local taxes to your city each year, they still insist on charging you for each disposal!

When you tell the *sodaigomi* people over the phone what it is you're throwing out they'll tell you how many special stickers you need to buy. You must buy these stickers from a local convenience store and place them on your item or else they'll refuse to take it. A sofa or a bed usually costs about ¥1,800 to dispose of, so if it's not broken you're probably better off uploading it to Craigslist or JMTY for someone to pick up for free.

If you can't find anyone who wants your stuff online, one alternative is to call your local recycle shop and see if they'll take it. Some moving companies may also do this for you. Depending on the item and its condition, they might do it for free, charge you a certain amount, or even pay you a little.

It should also be noted that if you're walking outside and see someone's *sodaigomi* stuff out on the street, you're not supposed to take it. Why not? Someone's just throwing it away, right? That's true, but the person has already paid money for their stickers, so Japanese people consider taking *sodaigomi* to be like stealing. To me this seems incredibly wasteful, but that's just the way things work here.

With all this in mind, only buy stuff you really like because you might be stuck with it a lot longer than you expected.

Avoiding Drama

Japanese apartments have much thinner walls than what you're likely used to. You'll be hearing your neighbors a lot more than you want to, and maybe inadvertently learn some things about them you never wished to learn. Or perhaps it's going to be you that causes people to complain. Playing loud music is normally very difficult in Japanese apartments without getting an immediate noise complaint. Also, I wouldn't recommend having any home parties. After seeing the size of a typical apartment, however, you probably wouldn't want to anyway. But that doesn't stop some people. If you're living in the same building with college students then get ready to put up with a lot of late night noise. This may be something you want to think about in advance when choosing a location.

Complaining in Japan, like many other things, is

often done indirectly. If you're making a lot of noise without realizing it, it's rare to have a neighbor come to your door directly, although this still might happen sometimes. You'll most likely hear about it from your management company the next day. Or if your music is too loud someone might even call the cops on you!

I've confronted my Japanese upstairs neighbors directly once when they were having a loud party at 3am on a weeknight and I had to work the next morning. I was polite about it, or at least as polite as someone who'd just been woken up for the 4th time that night could be. They apologized but continued the party just as loudly as before. I went over to complain a second time and eventually they quieted down. I never mentioned it to the landlord or anyone else, thinking that this would only result in more drama. All I wanted to do was get some sleep that night and I couldn't wait until the next day to complain.

Those neighbors didn't have any more parties after that, but I started to detect some strange behavior that I hadn't noticed before. For example, they started slamming their door extra hard when they entered and exited their apartment, and would start to talk in especially loud voices whenever they passed my door. Occasionally I would hear the word "*gaijin*" followed by some indecipherable muttering as they passed. You could call me paranoid, but Japanese do often tend to show their displeasure with you in subtle, passive aggressive ways. I thought I was taking the mature, adult course of action by politely confronting them in person without getting anyone else involved. But that's just not the way things are done here. Japanese generally prefer to snitch on each other and to be snitched on than to get involved in any type of direct confrontation, no matter how minor. This is something to keep in mind when living in a building with Japanese neighbors.

With that said, there are definitely some exceptions. You may have a neighbor who is incredibly direct, which in most cases will be an older Japanese male. I know a number of people, both Japanese and foreign, who receive regular angry calls or visits from their elderly neighbor for things as minor as their vacuum cleaner or washing machine being too loud, not to mention what happens when they have guests over. It's very difficult to tell who your neighbors are going to be when moving into a new place. If possible, try to aim for a building that has both few students and few retired people. Living in a unit surrounded by lots of offices may be your best bet.

Contract Renewal

Every two years you need to renew your lease if you want to keep living in your apartment. And yes, since this is Japan, there's going to be a fee for that. You'll typically need to pay a month's worth of rent along with insurance renewal fees. If your apartment is in the ¥60-80,000 a month range, expect to be paying over ¥100,000 in *addition* to your normal rent for that month! This will happen every two years and it's really important to be prepared for this in advance. Be sure to set some money aside ahead of time. If you really don't have the money then negotiating with your landlord or management company might be a possibility. Apparently this renewal fee is not so common in other regions of Japan like Kansai, but it's pretty much the standard in the Tokyo area.

11

SURVIVING EVERYDAY LIFE

There's a lot more to life than work. Your time away from your office or school is when you can finally relax and make the most of your life in this fascinating country. Just like when hunting for a job or finding an apartment, however, your foreigner status comes with its own set of difficulties and challenges. This chapter is meant to help you deal with certain aspects of daily life here on an emotional, physical and even legal level.

You Need a Hobby

Having a hobby of some sort is vital for your social and emotional wellbeing in Japan. For better or for worse, Japan is very much a society made up of groups and cliques. When you find yourself as an outsider, Japan can be an especially cold and alienating place. Once you're on the "inside," however, you'll find the people in your circle to be incredibly warm and welcoming. Becoming part of a group won't happen overnight but once you really get to know the people in your circle, they'll often turn into lifelong friends. I'm still close with Japanese friends that I met through the local music and arts scene in the city I lived in 6 or 7 years ago. Whenever I go back to visit it's as if nothing has changed.

You may enjoy a lot of your hobbies alone and at home, and while there's certainly nothing wrong with that, I highly recommend finding at least one hobby that involves going out and interacting with other like-minded people. If you have a hobby or passion already before coming to Japan then it's only a matter of seeking out that community wherever you live. If you're in the countryside, this may be more difficult unless your hobby is something specifically Japanese like judo or tea ceremony.

If you're looking for a new hobby that will allow you to make new friends and join a local community, here are some ideas:

- Join a local sports team
- Play in a band
- Train in the martial arts
- Join an ikebana, tea ceremony or calligraphy group
- Join a cooking class
- Get involved in a dancing community, such as hip hop, salsa or bellydancing

If you're into arts, music or cinema but don't necessarily produce anything yourself, simply just keep showing up at events or exhibitions. The Japanese people that are part of that scene will eventually remember your face and accept you as a regular.

Even in small cities there's often an "international group" which consists of foreign residents and English-speaking Japanese people who are well-travelled and interested in other cultures. Sometimes you can find foreign cultural events happening in your town, such as Chinese gyoza making or some kind of international song and dance performance. When you first get to Japan and don't speak much of the language, attending such events could be a quick and easy way to meet people. It might not do much to help your Japanese skills, however.

Japanese Medical Care

There are a lot of conflicting feelings among foreign residents on the quality of medical care in Japan. Some praise the friendliness and competence of the doctors and nurses while others have some real horror stories. It all depends on who you ask. Even after many years here my experience with medical care in Japan is relatively limited, as I prefer to avoid doctor visits unless absolutely necessary. However, I have some basic experience with general hospital visits, physical therapy, a dentist visit, acupuncture and a couple of very minor surgeries. Based on these experiences I also have some mixed feelings on the quality of Japanese medical care.

One thing I like about it is how many small clinics there are. There are plenty of large hospitals as well, but chances are you'll be living within an easy walking distance of a private clinic that specializes in whatever your problem is. Within a 5 or 6 minute walking distance from my apartment I have access to an orthopedic clinic, a dermatologist, a general practice clinic, a sports massage specialist, an acupuncturist, numerous dentists and one large hospital. I'm sure there are still more that I haven't even noticed.

Since hospitals and clinics receive most of their revenue from the national insurance system, their way of doing things is often based around being able to maximize these payments. Visit the dentist for a basic teeth cleaning, for example, and they'll finish cleaning your lower teeth and then tell you to come back another day for your uppers! This is a frustrating and inefficient way of doing things but it increases their insurance money. Remember that if you're on the national insurance program you'll still need to cover 30% of the cost yourself, and all those repeated visits can add up. Even if you don't have insurance, the annoying thing is that they'll make you come back another day to get the rest of your teeth cleaned anyway. Other people complain that they get kept in hospitals much longer than what seems reasonably necessary. This kind of thing is also often the result of the hospital trying to increase insurance revenue.

While I luckily haven't had any really scary or horrible experiences with medical care in Japan, one thing that bugs me is the arrogance of some of the doctors here. Most are quite courteous but they act more like your boss than someone who's sincerely trying to help you. They don't really respond well to patients second-guessing their diagnoses or methods of treatment. They'll often refuse to admit they were wrong even with new evidence to the contrary. I once had a mysterious problem with my leg that lasted for over half a year, making it very painful to walk for more than 20 minutes at a time. I visited a local clinic where the doctor confidently declared, within a few minutes of meeting me, that it was some kind of muscle problem. He then taught me a number of exercises to try every day. Despite visiting the clinic multiple times a week and doing the exercises every day for several months, there was zero improvement. To me it felt more like nerve pain. I kept trying to bring up this possibility with the doctor but he wouldn't hear any of it.

Frustrated, I stopped visiting the clinic and also stopped doing the exercises. I then did some intensive research online for side-effect free supplements that help with nerve problems. After ordering the supplements from iHerb.com and taking them for a month, the pain that I'd been experiencing for 7 or 8 months up to that point had finally subsided. This was long after I'd stopped doing the exercises. Had I continued visiting the clinic I would've wasted a lot more time and money on fixing this "muscle problem." I've also been misdiagnosed for other minor problems in the past, only to get prescribed strange medication that did nothing but make me feel sick and disoriented.

These experiences have not scared me away from Japanese medical care overall, as I've had other experiences that were quick, efficient and cost effective (even with no insurance). One place I will refuse to go back to, however, is the dentist. No, not just because of their annoying teeth cleaning policies but because I've personally met

3 people, one Japanese and two foreigners, who've had permanent mouth and jaw damage inflicted on them by Japanese dentists. Reading online forums, it seems that many others have also gone through similar experiences. Rather than take the risk, I prefer to travel abroad for treatment. If you're uninsured or just interested in some type of care or procedure that you're nervous about getting done in Japan, seeking out medical care in another Asian country is something you may want to consider.

Medical Tourism

Medical tourism, the act of flying abroad for cheap medical care, is becoming more and more common these days as medical standards in developing nations improve. Japanese generally don't do this as most people here don't speak English and the national health insurance system won't cover any care that one's deliberately travelled abroad for. For foreigners here, however, traveling to a nearby Asian country for a medical procedure might be worth looking into for a number of reasons.

The most obvious reason is language. English-speaking doctors in Japan do exist but they're usually at expensive private hospitals that may be out of your budget. It seems much easier to find affordable English-speaking practitioners in countries like Thailand, the Philippines, Malaysia, Taiwan or Korea.

The next reason would be cost. If you're not enrolled in the national health insurance program then you might actually save money by traveling abroad for medical care. This is after taking flight and accommodation costs into consideration. And I don't mean some primitive clinic located down a back alley, but a clean clinic or hospital with modern equipment and Western-educated doctors.

Another reason to consider medical tourism in Asia is quality. A lot of Westerners I talk to in Japan are dissatisfied with the level of medical care here. As I mentioned, I've had a mix of both good and bad experiences but I'm terrified of visiting a Japanese dentist for anything more than a cleaning. The other year when I needed to have a tooth filling refilled, I decided to visit a dentist in nearby Taiwan. The service was excellent. They were fluent in English, very professional and friendly, and the total cost was much lower than I'd expected. It was also a good excuse to do some sightseeing in a new country. I can't make the decision for you, but don't disregard medical tourism as an option if you're not happy with the level of service here.

Bringing Over Prescription Medication

If you're already on some type of prescription medication, be aware that you're not allowed to bring more than one month's supply into the country without filling out a special form. This form is called the "Yakkan Shomei" which can be downloaded at the Ministry of Health, Labour and Welfare's web site. The Yakkan Shomei is a type of import certificate and you need to fill it out in advance and show it to the customs officer when you arrive at the airport. A Yakkan Shomei is also required when receiving packages containing over a month's supply of prescription medication in the mail.

These laws also apply to contact lenses. I'd been having my family forward me packages of prescription contacts every several months for years until one day a package finally got snatched up by customs. I'd been totally unaware of the law or the Yakkan Shomei but they made me fill one out along with a copy of my prescription. I also had to travel to the other end of the city to pick up the package myself. Luckily, if you wear contact lenses then there's a better option. Visit the web site www.contactlens.co.jp (レンズダイレクト) where you can find a decent selection of lenses you can order with no prescription! (No, I have no association with them) They even had the brand my eye doctor in my hometown prescribed. It does sound kind of shady at first but for the past couple of years I've been wearing nothing but lenses ordered online and have had zero problems.

Being Vegetarian in Japan

To the dismay of many foreign residents and visitors, Japan just isn't a vegetarian-friendly country. Strict vegetarians may have to become somewhat flexible if they want to survive here long term. I've known a number of formerly dedicated vegetarians who eventually started eating fish and even chicken during their time in Japan, as the meat-free options were just too lacking. But some people do get by if they're willing to put in enough effort. This may entail occasionally skipping meals when there just aren't any other options.

While the Japanese aren't that big on eating thick steaks or huge burgers, they still eat plenty of meat. Just walk past any Yoshinoya or Matsuya at lunch time and notice how jam-packed with sweaty salarymen these places get. But surely Japan, with its strong Buddhist traditions and love of nature, has plenty of animal-free options, right? Whereas a lot of the food may appear vegetarian on the surface, the Japanese seem to have some kind of obsession with hiding an animal ingredient in nearly every dish or food product they prepare. This is sometimes easy to catch, like discovering bacon bits on your salad. Other meat products may be impossible to detect with the naked eye. Most of the noodle broth in Japan is either meat or fish-based and even miso soup contains dried fish flakes as an ingredient. Try explaining to your waiter that you're vegetarian, even in fluent Japanese, and they'll likely just give you a blank stare. Japanese restaurants are infamous for refusing to deviate even slightly from the predetermined menu, no matter how simple or easy the adjustment.

Vegetarian, vegan and organic restaurants are gradually increasing in places like Tokyo and Osaka but are still quite rare and mostly very expensive. There are a few reasonably priced restaurants out there, however, so I'd recommend doing an online search for vegetarian options in your area. The web site Happy Cow is an excellent resource. In certain business districts you may even come across a vegetarian food truck during lunch time and you'll almost never have to wait in line. Japan also has a large South Asian community and you'll surely find plenty of meatless options at your local Indian or Nepali restaurant. At the end of the day, vegetarians will just have to do their best to adjust to Japan until Japan can one day learn to accommodate vegetarians.

Racism and Xenophobia

Racism is still a big problem in Japan and it doesn't seem like it will ever go away. Before I continue, I should mention that most of my friends here are Japanese and I spend a lot more time speaking Japanese than I do English. Clearly, not all Japanese are racist and I've met a large number of genuinely compassionate and open-minded people who have been very kind and generous to me. If these people didn't exist then there's no way I would've stayed here for so long. But that still doesn't mean that I don't experience racism in daily life.

There are several obvious ways you'll know you're being discriminated against in Japan. For example, being denied housing, getting randomly stopped by the police, encountering a "Japanese only" sign or having a drunk old man tell you to get out of the country. Aside from these obvious examples, Japanese racism is generally much more indirect and subdued than in other cultures, to the extent that some newcomers even falsely believe that it's all a myth. It's not that these people are accepted while other foreigners are not. It's more likely they just haven't learned to decode all of the subtle signals yet.

First of all, on a daily basis you'll be forced to deal with a barrage of micro-aggressions. Prepare to get complemented on how well you can use chopsticks, even when the speaker knows you've lived here for years. You'll receive constant praise for your Japanese ability, even if you can only speak a couple of words. People generally don't have bad intentions when they make these comments and are expressing genuine surprise and fascination. They likely don't understand themselves that this fascination stems from a deeply rooted and racist belief that the Japanese are somehow special and that foreigners lack the intelligence to understand their language and culture. They react to a foreigner speaking fluent Japanese and using chopsticks in much the same way you or I would react to a dog that could speak English and use a fork and knife. Most long-term foreign residents don't want nor expect to be seen as a native Japanese, but certainly not as a completely different species either.

Other passive aggressive forms of racism are much more ill-intended yet harder to spot. You may notice how many people just happen to need to cough as soon as they walk by you and that the cough sounds very fake. Others will look you right in the eye as they bump into you on the street. A group of grown adults at the next table over in a restaurant will glance over at you and laugh. Old men and women will give you nasty stares in the supermarket. The bartender will insist on responding to your fluent Japanese in horribly broken English. In an exaggerated manner, people will sometimes pretend to act shocked and surprised when you walk by, even in a big city. Someone might stand extremely close to you in a queue or on an uncrowded subway, despite there being plenty of other space for them to stand. So what are you supposed to do about all of this? Due to the indirect nature of these acts, there's really nothing you can do, unfortunately. If you accuse a person of coughing on purpose when you walk by, they're only just going to tell you it was a real cough.

The worst situations are when you realize that an acquaintance or neighbor you thought you were friendly with has actually been subtly displaying their displeasure with you all along. Sometimes you may be talking to someone that at first seems like they're having a normal conversation with you in Japanese, but they're actually mocking you and talking down to you in a comedic way to look cool in front of their friends. Again, there's not much you can do about any of this except observe and learn. Once you know how to decode these signals, you'll know which people to avoid and who not to trust. Then you can focus your time and energy on hanging out with genuinely nice people.

Knowing the Laws

Suddenly immersing yourself in a new culture and being surrounded by a language you don't understand can be overwhelming and stressful. Some newcomers end up partying a little too hard in order to let off steam, while others feel that the language barrier itself gives them more freedom to say or do things they normally wouldn't back home. I'm not going to try and tell you how to live your lives, but over the years I've had several foreign acquaintances get themselves into deep trouble for a number of stupid reasons. Coming to Japan for the first time, it's important to inform yourself about the local laws and how they may effect you in everyday life.

Alcohol

Japan is strict and conservative in many regards but it's one of the most liberal countries in the world as far as alcohol is concerned. Drinking just about anywhere here is legal. Nobody will say anything if you drink a beer on the train or walk down a crowded street with a cup of sake, though it is somewhat frowned upon. Drinking is also a huge part of work culture. It's not uncommon to see a guy in a suit puking all over the sidewalk or asleep in a bush at 10:00pm on a Tuesday!

Drinking is acceptable in many situations outside the office but understand that Japan is especially tough on drunk drivers.

Tobacco

Smoking cigarettes is still legal and widely tolerated inside most bars, restaurants and nightclubs. If you absolutely can't stand cigarette smoke then Japan will drive you nuts. Oddly enough, you're forbidden from walking down the street with a cigarette or you could get fined, although I've never actually seen this happen to anyone. To buy cigarettes from a special tobacco vending machine you need a special ID card called a Taspo but you won't ever get carded purchasing tobacco products from a convenience store.

Drugs

Japan is very strict when it comes to drugs. They don't give drug users the death penalty like in Southeast Asia, but the penalties are still much harsher than in the West. Understand right away that the legal consequences of getting caught with something are much worse for foreigners than they are for Japanese. If you get caught with so much as a joint here you'll be given a very hard time, no matter if your name happens to be Paul McCartney.

Even if you yourself are clean, stay away from other people taking drugs. If you're with them when they get caught you'll also get in trouble for "witnessing a crime" and not reporting it. The police will consider you as an accomplice to this "crime"and prosecute you accordingly.

As a direct result of the strict drug laws in Japan, there's been a disturbing trend recently of chemically synthesized drugs being sold legally at head shops despite their harmful effects. They're referred to as *dappou haabu* and are meant to mimic the effects of cannabis. They're known as "loophole drugs" and the reason they can be sold legally is because once the government bans certain chemicals, someone just comes along and slightly alters the compounds. They then go and sell this new concoction before it's made illegal too, and the cycle continues to repeat itself. While possessing *dappou haabu* will not get you arrested, I highly recommend that you stay away from it. Not only is it terrible for your health but it just might mess you up enough to make you go ahead and commit a crime anyway, defeating the whole purpose of taking a "legal" drug in the first place.

Lastly, do not even think about trying to sell drugs in Japan. The very best that could happen to you if you get caught is lifetime deportation, but most likely you'll never be seeing the outside of a Japanese jail cell for many, many years. If you're so broke and desperate that you'd even be considering this then it's time to get the hell out of Japan.

Sex

Like most industrialized nations, the legal age of consent in Japan is 18.

In Japan, any sexual service aside from vaginal intercourse can legally be exchanged for money. There are sometimes even multiple red light districts within a single city. This is all technically legal and these businesses are almost entirely controlled by the yakuza. Openly being a member of the yakuza, by the way, is also legal in Japan.

Getting Stopped by The Police

As a foreigner in Japan, getting racially profiled by police is an unfortunate reality of life. You may be walking peacefully down the street one day, or coming out of the ticket gate at the train station, only to be stopped by one or two cops that demand you show them your ID. Sometimes they're polite about it and other times not so much. It's very important to keep in mind that as a foreigner, you are legally required to have your Residence Card on your person at all times.

This has happened to me several times over the years, though it's certainly not a weekly or even monthly occurrence. I've even had one awful experience in which I was about to enter a subway station when a cop aggressively grabbed my arm from behind and held onto it tightly. He demanded in front of everyone that I empty my pockets. Of course I had nothing on me and was let go. I was sober, but it was early morning and I wouldn't be surprised to learn that the cop himself had been drunk. I memorized his ID number which I demanded he show me before I complied. I called the local police headquarters when I got home to make a formal complaint but unsurprisingly, nothing came of it.

I know of other foreigners who've lived here for years without getting stopped while others have been stopped many more times than I have. The racial profiling is not only limited to foreigners, however. Some Japanese citizens also get stopped and asked to show their ID if they slightly "look foreign."

I'm caucasian but if you're of darker complexion expect it to happen fairly regularly. Sometimes outside of certain JR stations the cops will ignore me while stopping everyone that appears to be of South Asian or Middle Eastern descent. Never mind the fact that the only terrorist attacks to have taken place on Japanese soil have been perpetrated by Japanese citizens.

Officially, the cops should have an actual reason for stopping someone on the street but they usually make up some vague story about a foreigner committing a crime somewhere in the area. Due to this unspecified crime, they say, they must stop all non Japanese-looking people to confirm their identities. Even if their reason for stopping you is completely bogus, you do not want to get caught without your Residence Card.

What should you do if you get stopped? First of all, hopefully you have your card on you. I always make the cop show me their ID (not just badge) before I show anything of mine. They're legally required to do so and it's really the only thing you can do to give them a slight taste of their own medicine. Once they show you theirs, you've got to show them yours.

If you get stopped without your card, the police can legally detain you while they go to your home and search all over for it. That's something I'm sure most people would rather avoid, so make sure to always have your card on you. To prepare yourself for any potential problems with the local police there are some very useful online resources out there such as debito.org.

If you ride a bicycle you should also expect to get stopped. A lot. The cop will ask for the registration number of the bike and confirm it with someone over their walkie talkie to make sure it's not stolen. They don't normally check your ID though there is a small chance that they might. They do these checks for Japanese people too but as a foreigner you're a lot more likely to get stopped. Any number of times I've been riding my bicycle in the city together with Japanese friends, only for me to be the only one to get flagged down. I was once even stopped by a large group of cops who felt that 7 or 8 officers were necessary to confront a lone foreigner on a bicycle. In that very same neighborhood a week later, I witnessed a gangster beating up a taxi driver in plain view of the *koban* (police box) while the cop inside just sat there pretending not to see anything.

Another thing to keep in mind: If you're *gaijin* and you try to contact the police to report a crime, whether your own house was robbed or you witnessed something happen to a stranger, don't be surprised to be interrogated yourself as a potential suspect. For this reason, many foreign residents here don't dare contact the police even if they've had something stolen.

Avoiding Conflict

If you have some kind of scuffle or conflict with a Japanese person and the police get involved, you can bet that the cops, not to mention the courts and judges, are not going to be on your side. Violent crime in Japan is very rare in general but there have been some instances where Japanese nationals have assaulted foreigners and have gotten off completely clean. In some of these cases the perpetrator even admitted exactly what they did! I highly recommend avoiding getting into any type of argument or confrontation with a local that could potentially lead to violence. Even if someone shouts something racist at you in the street or on the train, it's best to just take a deep breath and walk away.

I know a few expats who've unexpectedly gotten

into physical altercations with people in the train station during rush hour which resulted in long and stressful lawsuits. As I mentioned, actual fights are rare, but shoving and intentionally knocking into people in crowded places are ways that some people here tend to let off steam in public. I've never been in a situation that turned violent but I have gotten into some tense stare downs and a few verbal altercations with rude people on station platforms or inside of trains. It's worth mentioning that I've been all over the country and these situations seem almost exclusively limited to Tokyo. If you're in a more well-mannered city then you shouldn't be too concerned. If something does happen wherever you are then it's vital to keep your cool.

Train Safety

On the subject of trains and arrests, Japan has a major problem with train gropers which are referred to as *chikan*. The problem is prevalent enough for there to be warning posters inside of train cars as well as verbal announcements. There are also special "women only" cars on certain train lines. If you're female and someone touches you, even if you don't speak Japanese, be sure to shout the word "*chikan!*" Everyone will know exactly what's going on. Hopefully some of the other passengers will help you restrain the pervert if he tries to run. At the next station, inform the train staff who will help you out and contact the authorities. The tricky thing is that trains, especially in Tokyo, can get extremely crowded and you may not always be able to detect a legitimate act of groping at first.

With that said, if you're a guy, make sure to be extra careful with your hands. If the train is packed, keep your hands on one of the poles or handles so that it's clear to those around you where they are. If you can't reach one, cross your arms or put your hands in your pockets. You definitely do not want to become an 'accidental *chikan*' on your way to work. There are occasional news stories of Japanese females falsely accusing guys on the train in order to extort money out of them. If you get arrested, you will have an extremely tough time proving your innocence without a number of witnesses vouching for you. Again, always be mindful of your hands during rush hour.

Getting Arrested

I've never been arrested in Japan and I hope things stay that way. Japan's justice system is notorious for its 99% conviction rate. It's not uncommon for someone to "confess" to a crime only for the actual criminal to get caught later on. As a foreigner, the entire process of getting arrested and interrogated is only going to be more confusing and intimidating than normal.

Understand that in Japan the police are legally allowed to detain someone for up to 23 days even **without charging them with a crime**. If you are arrested, expect to be detained for the entire 23 day period without bail. That's the norm and exceptions are incredibly rare. Remember, you are guilty until proven innocent.

When you first get arrested, Eric Yosomono of the

blog *Gaijinass* writes, "This initial interrogation will last late into the night and will involve several different officers [. .] You will most likely get to sleep an hour or so before you have to wake up and your second round of interrogation will begin that morning after a cold rice and boiled egg breakfast."

The police will likely try to get you to sign something and tell you that as soon as you sign, "you can go home once they have 'cleared everything up.' [. . .] **These are lies, a tactic to trick you and nothing else.**"[32] This document is likely a confession and if you later tell a judge that you were lied to about what you signed, it won't matter. The interrogation process will not be videotaped and it's not unusual for your interrogators to get physical with you. All this torture can stop, your interrogators will tell you, if you just sign a simple document.

Detainees often feel they have no way of winning even if they really are innocent. For this reason, many give false confessions so they can finally end these tortuous interrogations. Furthermore, showing remorse in Japan is one of the key ways to receive a lighter punishment. Innocent suspects will often go ahead and show remorse for their "crime" in front of the judge. Accordingly, repeatedly proclaiming innocence may even result in a harsher punishment. If you regularly follow the news here, the "I was really drunk and don't remember a thing" excuse is also a very popular choice.

When dealing with police you'll have an easier time if you only speak in English. It doesn't matter how good your Japanese skills are. In fact, it would be in your best interest to keep your Japanese knowledge a secret.

Once they see you're willing to speak in their language, they may expect you to cooperate and understand everything in Japanese from that point on, clearly giving them the upper hand. "Demand that you receive an interpreter," writes Arudou Debito. "Hold out for one."[33]

Please, use basic common sense and follow some of my advice in the previous section to avoid ever getting arrested in the first place.

12

LEARNING THE LANGUAGE

When you first arrive in Japan it won't be long at all before you realize how poor the standard of English is in this country. Consequently, it's imperative that you put in the effort to learn the local language in order to get the most out of your Japan experience. Not only do you want to be able to get by and carry out your daily tasks with ease, but Japanese fluency is also vital for making friends and becoming part of your local community.

In the early days, your employer will help you out with a lot of things and in the bigger cities there are plenty of English-speaking businesses which target the expat community. I'm not saying you're going to starve or anything if you don't pick up the language. You may even come across expats who've lived in Japan for 15 years and can hardly utter a complete sentence in Japanese. Keep in mind that these people are often entirely reliant on someone else, often their spouse or employer. Acquiring Japanese is necessary if you want to not just survive here but to have as much control over your own life as possible.

This begs the question, however - how much Japanese do you actually need? It's clearly a very difficult language to learn and it's not something you're just going to pick up in a couple of months. You may get good enough to conduct basic conversations about the weather fairly early on but it's probably going to take at least a couple years of constant study and practice before reaching what's known as "business-level" fluency. In the end, it all depends on what your goals are. While I think everyone ought to become at least conversationally fluent, some foreigners may have a lot more use for advanced Japanese than others. In any case, I recommend you start studying the basics from as early on as possible. The purpose of this chapter is not to teach you the language but to give you an idea of what you're in for as you start down the long and bumpy road of Japanese language study.

Reading and Writing

Before even stepping foot in the country, I recommend memorizing both the hiragana and katakana alphabets, along with some basic conversational phrases you'll need for daily tasks. If you're completely new to the language, it's important to know that Japanese has three written alphabets. Hiragana and katakana are both phonetic alphabets that are unique to Japan. Both of these alphabets contain 48 letters each and are not too difficult to memorize after a few weeks of daily study. Katakana is used for phonetically spelling out loan words from other languages (in most cases English). As a foreigner, you'll need katakana to spell out your own name and if you see katakana on a restaurant menu, chances are it's spelling out a word you already know. If you only have time to learn one alphabet before coming here, katakana is going to be of more use to you in the short-term.

Japanese also uses kanji, or Chinese characters. One of the most difficult things about Japanese kanji is that one character often has 3 or 4 different pronunciations depending on context and what other kanji it's being combined with. Kanji is not something you learn in a few months. It's very much a lifelong learning process. With that said, starting to learn basic elementary school level kanji and memorizing a couple a day is a great habit. I especially recommend memorizing the kanji for places in your local city or prefecture. Train stations don't always have English letters on the route maps, although they may sometimes have hiragana written above the kanji names.

Speaking and Pronunciation

While reading and writing are important, conversational Japanese will be much more useful to you in everyday life and the learning process is also a lot quicker. Even if you study kanji for years, you probably still won't be able to read a basic newspaper article and understand even half of it. Working on your conversational skills will get you a lot further in that same amount of time. After a couple years of practice you should at least be able to have a basic discussion about the topic of that same newspaper article.

Japanese has a grammatical structure very different from that of English and of course the vocabulary is also completely different, not taking loan words into account. It's not as intimidating of a language to learn as many people would think, however. First of all, pronunciation is easy. Contrary to common belief, Japanese is not a tonal language like Chinese. If you can pronounce words in Spanish then you already know most of the basic vowel and consonant sounds. Next, verb conjugations are much simpler than most European languages. There are only a couple of tenses and the verb forms don't change regardless of whether the subject is *I, you, she, us* or *they*. Noun genders are also nonexistent. You've likely come across tricky particles like *wa, ga, ni* or *he* if you've studied the language before. Well, good news. In spoken Japanese it's not technically incorrect to just leave these out of the sentence!

As mentioned above, pronunciation is pretty straightforward in Japanese, but that doesn't mean you're going to sound like a native right away. One of the most frustrating things about speaking Japanese as a foreigner is that you'll often struggle to figure out the 'Japanese' pronunciation of an English loan word. Most Japanese people won't have any idea of what you're saying unless you use the exact katakana pronunciation which often sounds ridiculous to native speakers. Despite everyone knowing what 'Hello Work' is for example, people here will only be able to understand you if you pronounce it their way: *Harou Waaku*. Some other notable examples are "stew" pronounced as *shichuu* and "virus" pronounced as *uirusu*. As an English teacher, trying to teach proper pronunciation of these loan words is pretty much futile. The students will only go home to hear that word repeated over and over again on TV in the katakanized pronunciation.

Keigo

Something you'll encounter in Japanese study that you won't find often in Western languages is the use of *keigo*, or honorific speech. The most difficult aspect of *keigo* is not learning how to use it, but *when* to use it. This is something that even causes native Japanese a lot of anxiety. To make matters even more confusing, there are multiple levels of *keigo*. It's often used just to be polite but its real purpose is to reinforce social hierarchy. Therefore, just because one person is using *keigo*, it doesn't always mean that the other person is going to use it back!

The first form of polite speech you'll come across is the kind that changes the end of verbs to *-masu* and ends sentences with *-desu*. This is called *teineigo*. In daily life you'll be using it a lot. It's often just used by default when talking to someone for the first time or when communicating with anyone you're still not very familiar with. If that person is around your age, you'll naturally shift to plain, informal Japanese as you become more friendly with each other. This often happens within minutes of the conversation. In other cases you may think you're getting to know someone quite well but realize they're still using *keigo* with you. There's no exact way to pinpoint why and it often just depends on the person. It could be because they're still not completely comfortable with you or because they're slightly younger than you and think of you as their *senpai*. I even know some people who use *keigo* when speaking with younger acquaintances, although that's considered fairly abnormal.

As I mentioned, a major aspect of *keigo* etiquette is age. If you're a junior high school teacher, for example, and some of your students are part of the same brass band or judo club, there will naturally be a mix of different grades. The younger students will use *keigo* with the older students, even if the age difference is only one year. The older students will instead use plain speech in return. I thought this was kind of cute at first until I discovered that this social dynamic lasts well into adulthood. I've seen many instances of adults in their 20's and 30's use *keigo* with their own close friends just a year or two their senior. In contrast, I've also seen pairs of friends that use plain speech with each other even with an age gap of several years between them. This phenomenon is something I still don't really understand after all my time here. And after having asked many Japanese people about it, it seems that they don't even fully understand it either.

If you find yourself in a business situation, you'll have to use honorific forms that extend way beyond -*masu* and -*desu*. Instead of *desu*, for example, the sentence might end with -*de gozaimasu*. In other cases, certain verbs and nouns might change completely. Even Japanese workers go through training on how to use this type of business speech properly. While you likely won't need to use business speech as a newcomer or as an English teacher, you'll be exposed to it often as a customer at a store. If you have the time then it might be worth going over the basics. After having lived in Japan for a couple of years and considering yourself fairly fluent, it can be a humbling experience to go get a new cell phone or order bus tickets and have no idea what the other person is saying!

Useful Resources

- The most popular textbook series for learning Japanese is the *Genki* **series**. This is where I'd start studying the language as an absolute beginner. Each section contains a dialog to help you understand important grammar points and there's also a CD included for listening comprehension. *Genki* produces a separate work book for each level that you can use for extra practice. Admittedly, I haven't picked up a *Genki* textbook in over ten years so the details aren't very fresh in my mind. But I remember it being very helpful when I first started studying the language and it's nice to see that it's still just as popular today.

- A great kanji practice workbook for beginners is *Kanji Power* by John Millen. There's space inside the book for writing practice and a number of example sentences are given for each kanji.

- As far as apps go, I most often use the app simply

titled "**Japanese**," developed by Spacehamster. It's my regular go-to dictionary but it also contains JLPT vocabulary and study flashcards if you want to brush up on your vocab on the train. It's available for both Android and iOS.

- Considering how I started learning Japanese and hiragana long before our modern smartphone era, I don't have any experience with apps for beginners, but I do hear good things about **Mirai Japanese** and **Learn Japanese** by MindSnacks.

- For high beginner or intermediate students, the book *Making Sense of Japanese* by Jay Rubin (who's known for translating some of Haruki Murakami's novels) is a great read. Rubin breaks down the subtle differences between things like *wa* and *ga* and the correct grammatical usage of words like *hodo* and *tame*.

- I also recommend downloading the *rikaichan* or *rikaikun* plugins for your web browser, which automatically translate the Japanese words you hover over with your mouse. The information shows up instantaneously in a little pop-up box so it won't interrupt your browsing experience. You can also see the hiragana pronunciation of any kanji that you hover over. Be careful, though, as you can quickly get into the habit of relying on the plugins instead of making the effort to memorize the words.

- A lot of people learn Japanese by **reading manga**. That's not really my thing and I've never read a manga in my life, but if that's one of your interests then it could be a powerful study tool. **Watching Japanese movies** or dramas in their original language will help improve your listening skills and demonstrate how the example dialogues in textbooks aren't always how people really talk.

- There are also an enormous amount of free **YouTube** videos out there for all skill levels. While I think taking private lessons is the best way to go, we're very lucky to be living in an era where thousands of free videos and other online resources are right there at our fingertips.

Language, Otherness and Dating

Many expats wonder how much of the language they'll need to learn before they can date and start a relationship with a Japanese person. This is very much case-by-case and it obviously depends on the English level of the other person. Newcomers are often eager to study and improve their language skills so they can try out some new phrases on that cute girl or guy at the bar. In some cases, however, language ability can actually work against you.

There are a lot of Japanese, especially women, who are attracted to foreigners mainly because of their exoticness or "otherness." Due to this mentality, many foreigners interested in short flings may actually have better success the less Japanese they know. Once they start using fluent Japanese, they automatically lose some of their otherness and no longer have the same appeal they once had to these "*gaijin* hunters." On the other hand, when meeting members of the opposite sex who are not so shallow and who are actually willing to see you as an individual, the more Japanese you know the better.

Language and Cultural Defense Mechanisms

Japanese people are often taken aback when encountering a foreigner that speaks fluent conversational Japanese. The Japanese grow up hearing over and over again that their language is the most difficult in the world to learn. This makes them feel unique and special and it's something they take great pride in. When a foreigner is able to speak fluently, some Japanese may even become defensive, as if you've penetrated right through their sacred cultural space. When Japanese feel defensive like this they might try to create more cultural or social distance between them and you, often indirectly by using compliments.

You may be talking with someone about current events, your favorite cafe in Kyoto or the latest political scandal, when several minutes into the conversation they might suddenly say: "Your Japanese is really good. Did you study in your home country before you came here?" Sure, this sounds like a harmless compliment, and it would be if they said it an appropriate time, *i.e*, not right in the middle of your sentence about a completely different topic. This happens to me very often when talking with someone I haven't already known for awhile. People may not realize consciously what they're doing, but I see these interruption / compliment hybrids as that person's way of saying: "Having this normal conversation with a *gaijin* in *my* own language is really freaking me out!" This is one reason that I feel little motivation to become more fluent than I currently am. I see little benefit in attaining native-level Japanese ability when people here are only going to be paying more attention to the color of my skin than the actual words coming out of my mouth.

Language and Employment

When you first come to Japan you'll probably be teaching English. Japanese language ability is almost never required for English teaching jobs, so don't feel pressured to be fluent by the time you get to your interview. With that said, language ability is often respected because it shows that you're dedicated to living in Japan. If you're applying for a job where you'll be around non-English speaking Japanese staff, showing off your Japanese skills can put you ahead of some of the other candidates. Some ALT companies may test your language ability to determine how well you'll be able to get along with the other teachers in the staff room. I've even once been interviewed entirely in

Japanese for an eikaiwa job, despite everyone at the workplace being fluent in English. I'm still not really sure why they did this but they did give me an offer in the end.

Beyond teaching, many other jobs are going to require at least conversational or business-level Japanese ability. Some jobs even may require native fluency. As I went over in Chapter 9, certain professions require special business licenses for which you need to pass an exam that was created with only native speakers in mind. On the other hand, employers in the IT sector, for example, will likely appreciate Japanese ability but it's going to be your specific skill set and abilities that get you noticed in the first place. Even if you study the language for years and years and achieve native-level ability, you may still struggle to find work if you lack the skills that employers in your field are looking for. Again, it all depends on what it is you want to do with your life, but there are only so many hours in a day. I recommend finding a balance between your Japanese language study and leveling-up the skills you need to get your dream job.

The JLPT

For jobs that openly require a certain level of Japanese ability, you'll usually be asked which level of the Japanese Language Proficiency Test, or JLPT, you've passed. There used to be only 4 levels but a fifth was added the other year - a new Level N3 in between N2 and the old N3. N1 is the most difficult, with N5 being the easiest. To be considered "native" by an employer you need to have passed N1, or *1-kyuu*. This, in theory, means that you know all the kanji and vocabulary that a final year Japanese high school student knows. After N1, N2 is the only other level that has any real significance when hunting for a job, and it usually means that you have what's considered "business level" Japanese. Passing either of these top 2 levels requires years of study and dedication. But is a JLPT certificate really worth it?

    I've never taken the JLPT N1 or 2 myself. This is simply because I've never tried to join a company that required it. By now I've worked outside of the ESL industry for longer than I've worked in it and I've been doing fine without a JLPT certificate. Again, it all depends on what you want to do. If a high JLPT score is necessary to get the job of your choice then make passing the test one of your life goals. Don't confuse having passed the JLPT N1 with perfect fluency, however. As the exam doesn't test your speaking ability, there are even some people out there who've passed the JLPT N1 but can hardly carry on a natural-sounding conversation. If you're still unsure of what you want to do, I personally feel that developing advanced conversational fluency is a better goal to have. With good speaking skills you can form a lot of connections with people who could potentially introduce you to some great opportunities down the road.

The Usefulness of Japanese

Even though I strongly recommend developing your Japanese skills for a number of reasons, there are also some arguments against getting too deep into it. I already mentioned how you're always going to be considered an outsider and when the Japanese hear you speaking fluently, they often react how you or I might react to a dog speaking fluent English. If that weren't discouragement enough, you should also realize that the language is pretty much useless as soon as you step foot off the island. Learning Japanese and then leaving Japan would be like learning how to cattle graze before moving to a big city. It's just not a skill you can take with you many places.

When I travel outside Japan I often feel that spending as much time as I have to learn Japanese was maybe a mistake. Don't get me wrong - it's helped me tremendously in my everyday life and I never would've lasted so long here without it. But what use is my Japanese going to be once I move away? If I'd put the same amount of effort into studying Spanish or Chinese instead, I'd have a lot more opportunities to use those skills internationally. In touristy areas abroad I even overhear much more Korean than I do Japanese. Japanese expat communities in cities like New York or London, from my experience, tend to stay in their own little bubbles and don't mix very much with the locals.

Unless you have excellent Japanese skills that you

can use for some kind of business once you leave the country, there's really not much you can do with it other than keep in touch with your friends back on the island. This realization is one reason why many expats often get "hooked" here. They don't want to waste all the hard work and effort they've put into language study. I've even moved away and come back a couple of times myself. Of course, wanting to reunite with my friends and my enjoyment of the lifestyle were the main reasons, but I think there was also a subconscious fear of letting my Japanese ability go to waste that partly influenced my decisions. I've finally learned to accept the harsh reality of the matter, however. Since I don't intend to stay here forever, I've been putting more of my time and energy into studying Spanish, a much more useful and versatile language.

I don't mean to contradict myself and I still say that you ought to study and work hard on improving your Japanese skills if you're going to live in Japan. But do you have a clear idea of what it is you want to do here and does it require a very high level of Japanese? If not, then once you reach conversational fluency, you'd be better off developing other skills that are likely to provide a better return on investment.

13

UNDERSTANDING THE JAPANESE

In many ways, Japan appears fairly Western on the surface. You can drink a Starbucks coffee just about anywhere, watch baseball on TV or hear American pop music played in most department stores. Beneath the surface, however, there are some very significant cultural differences that aren't always going to be obvious to the newcomer. Even if you're only going to be living here for a year or two, having a basic understanding of some key Japanese cultural concepts will help you make sense of certain situations that may baffle you at first.

It's All About the *Wa*

The concept of *wa* is one of the most important characteristics of Japanese culture and society. It dictates the way people interact, express their feelings and react to problems. A major reason why Japan is such a safe country with so little violent crime is thanks to *wa*, generally translated into English as "harmony." The Japanese idea of a harmonious society is one without conflict and where individuals make personal sacrifices for the benefit of the group. One consequence of *wa* that you'll notice early on is how people tend to hold back from expressing opinions that could be considered even remotely controversial. Self-expression, individuality and even personal happiness are sometimes things that must be sacrificed for the sake of "harmony."

If you ever do business with a Japanese person they can often appear to be incredibly indecisive. They're not just trying to decide on the best course of action business-wise, but a decision that won't ruffle the feathers of their superiors or the people at company headquarters. Many Japanese businesses will even avoid making decisions that might upset their own competitors too much. *Wa* has an incredible influence over Japanese business culture and if you're going to be working here, it's a topic I suggest you read up on.

Honne and *Tatemae*

Honne is how you really feel about something while *tatemae* is how you express yourself for the sake of maintaining the *wa*. *Tatemae* has both positive and negative connotations. While all Japanese (and humans everywhere, really) are *tatemae* at work or while speaking with someone new, some people just seem to be in *tatemae* mode all the time. If you're new to Japan, this can be difficult to detect at first and you may just assume that person is naturally friendly and polite. While *tatemae* is necessary in certain situations, even Japanese don't like those who are *tatemae* too often.

Calling someone *tatemae* is equivalent to calling them "two-faced" in the West. Considering how people are often *tatemae* at work, I'd hesitate to be too *honne* with your Japanese colleagues until you're absolutely sure you can trust them. Despite acting friendly and sympathetic on the surface, they may very well be repeating everything you say to upper management behind your back. I think one reason the Japanese talk about food so much is not just because they love food, but because it's such a safe, non-controversial topic. Two people can discuss their different tastes in food without disturbing the *wa*. If a coworker gossips behind your back about how you said you preferred salmon over tuna, no one's going to care. If you find yourself in a Japanese working environment, be prepared to talk about food and the weather. A lot.

Real, genuine people who aren't afraid to express their opinions do exist in Japan. I know plenty of Japanese with whom I can get into all sorts of discussions about politics or other potentially sensitive topics. You just need to actively seek these *honne* people out.

Uchi and *Soto*

The *uchi-soto* paradigm refers to "us and them," or literally "inside-outside." As Japan is an extremely group-oriented culture, *uchi* refers to those within your inner circle while *soto* is everyone on the outside. Naturally, an individual is often part of many groups in their lifetime: a family, a company, a sports team, etc. The *uchi* mentality shifts accordingly depending on the situation.

In group situations, the Japanese are known for being well-mannered and incredibly polite. Walk through a crowded station in Tokyo, however, and notice how many people act as if those around them simply don't exist. People regularly block crowded staircases as they stare down at their cellphones without a care in the world. Others bump right into each other without even making eye contact or saying "excuse me." Driving manners are not much better and I've almost been run over any number of times. This is the result of people's *uchi* consisting only of themselves at that moment.

In everyday life, true harmony and togetherness are rarely felt on a larger societal level. If you're not part of some group or organization then you're basically a nobody. It's also rare for people to interact with strangers in public. The Japanese seem to only really feel united as one people when comparing themselves with the outside world. You'll find lots of television programs comparing Japanese cuisine or culture with that of another country, reminding the viewers daily that Japan is unique and special. This is known as *nihonjinron*. You'll also notice how international sports competitions are incredibly popular here, even if it's a sport that nobody really likes. I rarely meet any pro volleyball enthusiasts, for example, but whenever the Japanese team is in a big tournament, it's all over TV. International sporting events are one of the rare chances the Japanese get to feel like the entire nation is *uchi*.

Uchi and *soto* also have a literal connotation, referring to the inside and outside of one's home. The reason you need to take off your shoes when visiting someone's house is to avoid contaminating the realm of *uchi* with any of the dirt that came from *soto*.

Understand that as a foreigner, you will never, ever become part of the *uchi* of Japanese society as a whole, even if you become a naturalized citizen. (*Gaijin* literally means "outside person.") You can, however, eventually be accepted into the *uchi* of a particular group or social circle, which I highly recommend pursuing.

Senpai and *Kohai*

Group harmony does not come without rigid social hierarchy, at least not in Japan. Within a group setting, people are extremely conscientious of who is above or below them on the social ladder. This greatly effects how they interact with one another and what they talk about. Maintaining the *wa* is less about making sure everyone is happy than it is about pleasing one's superiors. Observe a small group of salarymen at the *izakaya* and within a couple of minutes you should be able to figure out who the leader, or *senpai*, is. Often it's the guy making corny jokes while the others compete to see who can laugh the loudest.

If you teach at a public school in Japan you'll see how the *senpai-kohai* dynamic works in a school setting. Younger students will use polite speech, or *keigo*, when talking to their upperclassmen even just one year their senior. This is especially prevalent in extracurricular clubs. In a martial arts club, for example, you might see the younger students diligently cleaning the dojo while the older students give them orders. It's not so one-sided, however, as the older students act as the mentors, teaching those with less experience the proper forms and techniques.

The *senpai-kohai* dynamic, in its ideal form, is akin to a master-apprentice relationship but with multiple people involved. The *senpai* are supposed to teach, guide and look after their *kohai*. The problem with *senpai-kohai*, however, is that the roles are determined by age and experience and not by actual talent or ability. What happens when the *kohai* is clearly more talented than their *senpai*? I've seen this first-hand many times, whether we're talking about a school judo club, local music scene or typical corporate office. Regrettably, the younger person often holds back to avoid upstaging and potentially embarrassing their *senpai*. As the age gap will always be there, this social dynamic will never change. The end result is a major waste of talent. It's no wonder why so many gifted young Japanese feel the need to go abroad to find success.

Giri

Giri means "duty" or "obligation." It refers to an individual's obligation to their group or to society as a whole. In a Japanese family, the parents are obligated to care for their children no matter what. This is why *hikikomori* recluses don't get kicked out of the house. It's also common for Japanese men or women to continue living with their parents until marriage, even into their thirties or forties. Likewise, when the parents get older or become ill, it then becomes the child's duty to care for them in return.

As mentioned, Japan is a society with very little violent crime, but a lot of the tragic stories you read about in the news are unfortunately disputes between relatives. Please understand that I am *not* saying these are normal or typical occurrences. In some extreme cases, however, the sense of *giri* to care for a family member can cause so much stress and pressure that the end result is sometimes violent. A number of these cases involve a son or daughter who walked away from a lucrative career in order to take care of an ailing parent full-time. Retirement communities in Japan do exist but they're not nearly as prevalent as they are in the West.

The concept of *giri* has also greatly influenced the Japanese culture of gift giving. Whenever people go on trips, even if only for a day or two, it's a cultural obligation to bring back souvenirs for everyone in one of their inner circles. If you receive a gift from a Japanese person they'll usually expect you to return the favor eventually. On Valentine's Day, women give "*giri* chocolate" to their male coworkers while a month later those men are expected to give back white chocolate in return. Foreign residents in Japan often criticize the practice and argue that gifts should be given from the heart and not out of a sense of obligation. I've brought this up with some Japanese friends who did not entirely disagree. Societal norms, they pointed out, make spontaneous displays of affection very difficult for some people. Therefore, a lot of Japanese appreciate the formalities of *giri* culture because it allows them to show appreciation for others in a way that doesn't make everyone feel awkward.

Gaman

The concept of *gaman* is considered to be one of Japanese culture's greatest virtues. *Gaman* is endurance, self-restraint, patience and diligence all rolled into one. After World War II, the Japanese didn't sit around whining and complaining, but endured their hardships and built up the country to become the economic powerhouse it is today.

The term can also be used for situations in everyday life. Really craving just one more piece of cake but know you've already had enough? Just *gaman*. Have an important work meeting but suddenly came down with a cold? Well, *gaman* through it and get it done. Playing in the final of a baseball tournament with a sore shoulder? Just *gaman* and you'll be fine!

Gaman is generally a positive term, but it also has an ugly side. The Japanese often consider the act of *gaman* itself to be virtuous, even if the very thing they are enduring is unfair and unjust. As a result, you'll rarely ever see anyone standing up for themselves. It's almost as if some people actually *like* their horrible working conditions and unpaid overtime, so that when they finally get home at 1AM they can pat themselves on the back for being able to *gaman* through it all.

"Shou ga nai"

"*Shou ga nai*" or "*Shikata ga nai*," which both mean the same thing, are phrases that are very closely related to *gaman*. Both phrases can be translated to "It can't be helped." Something gets in your way that you can't control, like unexpected weather, illness or technical issues? Just say "*Shou ga nai*" and keep moving forward!

Like *gaman*, "*shou ga nai*" has both a positive and negative aspect. The problem with "*shou ga nai*" is that the Japanese use it all the time when there's something they just don't feel like dealing with, even if it's very much within the realm of human control. "Look, I know the way we've been doing things up until now hasn't been working out," your coworker might say. "But we can't make any adjustments now. That would just be too difficult and confusing. *Shou ga nai, ne*." The attitude behind "*shou ga nai*" is the reason nothing ever really changes in this country. Trust me, you will be hearing this phrase a lot.

Your Place as a Foreigner

The concept of *wa* deserves credit for a lot of Japan's positive aspects, such as safety, orderliness, cleanliness and punctuality. On the other hand, the *wa* can be pretty damn oppressive at times, especially if you're a staunch individualist like me. Even many Japanese that have lived abroad have a hard time transitioning back, as they find all the social rules and overall tense atmosphere of Japan to be too much for them. They may have lived half their lives in a foreign country but they're still expected to play by all the rules once they return. As a *gaijin*, however, how many of these social concepts and rules will actually apply to you? As a foreign resident, what is your role, if any, within Japan's "harmonious society?"

As I mentioned earlier, you will never be regarded as a regular member of society here. If you try too hard to follow all of the social rules, the Japanese will only get defensive and create more distance between them and you. Don't try at all, however, and the locals won't respect you. Living a fulfilling life here as a foreigner is all about knowing when to live by the *wa* and when not to.

As someone who's just arrived and doesn't speak a lick of Japanese, nobody's going to expect you to understand things like *wa* or *tatemae* or *giri* at all. While physically present in Japan, it will almost be as if you exist on another plane of reality. Some foreigners enjoy this status because it means they can get away with a lot of stuff they wouldn't be able to back home. They might act a little wild and crazy or commit any number of cultural faux pas, knowing they'll be forgiven as a *gaijin* who doesn't, or just couldn't, know any better. Take advantage of this too much and it only gives all other gaijin a bad name, however. It's important that you embrace the social freedoms you have as a foreigner in Japan while still being sensible and responsible.

Expats who remain on the outside for too long

usually end up feeling isolated and depressed. This is another reason why it's vitally important to integrate into society to at least *some* degree. Learn Japanese, demonstrate good manners and show respect for the culture. But also don't be too afraid to be yourself. You're always going to be seen as different no matter what you do so you might as well embrace it. Some Japanese like hanging out with foreigners because they get to hear real, down-to-earth thoughts and opinions that they might not get out of their Japanese peers. Take advantage of this.

One thing I like about being a *gaijin* is that I can make friends of all ages while disregarding the whole *senpai-kohai* dynamic. Once I become familiar with someone, I usually insist on using plain speech even if they're older than me. It's not out of disrespect but simply because I feel that if I'm going to be good friends with someone, we should get artificial social barriers like *keigo* out of the way. Conversely, I tell younger friends not to use keigo with me. I think some people actually find this refreshing and it puts them at ease.

Another benefit of being a foreigner is that you can more easily drift between different scenes or social circles, belonging to two or more at a time. Japanese people generally tend to stick with one social group depending on their hobby, and they also feel a certain sense of *giri* to this group. They make a conscious effort to show up to social functions as much as possible, almost as if it were a second job. If you have a number of different hobbies and interests, however, feel free to get involved with different groups. Go ahead and distribute your time evenly among each one. As a foreigner, people will be a lot more forgiving in this regard. The one big exception, of course, would be work. You don't ever want to skip those *nomikai*s or company parties, as torturous as they can sometimes be.

Once you start integrating into society a bit more, you will also inevitably encounter certain people with whom you can just never win. The better language skills you demonstrate, the more pressure they'll put on you to follow all the social rules and customs, constantly reminding you that "This is Japan." Do everything perfectly just as a Japanese would, however, and those same people will go out of their way to exclude you because you'll never be one of them. You'll come across any number of these toxic people during your time here and it's in your best interest to avoid them if you can. Search for more open-minded friends that are willing to accept and appreciate you as an individual.

In summary, if you play things right, you can make a lot of local friends while also getting to live more or less by your own rules, reaping the benefits of being both *uchi* and *soto* at the same time. Foreigners who manage to find this sweet spot end up having a very hard time pulling themselves away from this place.

Conclusion

Making the leap to come over to Japan and earn a living is not going to be easy. But it can definitely be accomplished with enough knowledge and the right attitude.

Some people quickly find out that Japan is not for them and go home after a couple of months. On the other hand, others come intending to stay for only a year but find themselves sticking around for 20 or more. Even with all its setbacks and difficulties, living in Japan can be an incredibly rewarding experience and it's no wonder why so many foreigners find it difficult to leave.

I really hope this book has helped you in some way and I wish you the best of luck on your new journey. If you have any questions or comments, you can reach me at startyourlifeinjapan@gmail.com and I'll do my best to get back to you when I can.

Notes

1. "Studying in Japan." Japan Guide. Accessed February 28, 2016. http://www.japan-guide.com/e/e2232.html.
2. "Working Holiday Visa F.A.Q | Japan Association for Working Holiday Makers." Working Holiday Visa F.A.Q | Japan Association for Working Holiday Makers. Accessed February 28, 2016. http://www.jawhm.or.jp/eng/visa_faq.html.
3. "FAQ." The Official Website of the JET Program USA. 2014. Accessed February 28, 2016. http://jetprogramusa.org/faq/.
4. Richey, Michael. "How to Apply for the JET Program - Tofugu." Tofugu. Accessed February 28, 2016. http://www.tofugu.com/guides/how-to-apply-for-the-jet-program/.
5. Richey, Michael. "JET Program Statement of Purpose Guide - Tofugu." Tofugu. Accessed February 28, 2016. http://www.tofugu.com/guides/how-to-write-the-jet-program-statement-of-purpose-essay/.
6. "Driving a Car." Japan Guide. Accessed February 28, 2016. http://www.japan-guide.com/e/e2022.html.
7. "Driving a Car." Japan Guide. Accessed February 28, 2016. http://www.japan-guide.com/e/e2022.html.
8. Otake, Tomoko. "Japan Pension System Hacked; 1.25 Million Cases of Personal Data Leaked." Japan Times. June 01, 2015. http://www.japantimes.co.jp/news/2015/06/01/national/crime-legal/japan-pension-system-hacked-1-25-million-cases-personal-data-leaked/.
9. Patton, Mike. "The Seven Most Indebted Nations." Forbes. September 29, 2014. http://www.forbes.com/sites/mikepatton/2014/09/29/the-seven-most-indebted-nations/#5df3bee32cb3.
10. McCrostie, James. "Harassers Exploit Gaba's 'man-to-man' Lesson Format | The Japan Times." Japan Times. June 16, 2014. http://www.japantimes.co.jp/community/2014/06/16/issues/harassers-exploit-gabas-man-man-lesson-format/.

11. Lang, Martin. "Shane Schools Japan - Know What You're Letting Yourself in for." ESL Teachers Board. Accessed February 29, 2016. http://www.eslteachersboard.com/cgi-bin/asia/index.pl?read=786.

12. "Coco Juku." Tozen. March 18, 2014. http://tokyogeneralunion.org/category/coco-juku/.

13. "Business Practices at Winbe." The Truth About Winbe. Accessed February 29, 2016. http://winbe0.tripod.com/id20.html.

14. Currie-Robson, Craig. "For Japan's English Teachers, Rays of Hope amid the Race to the Bottom." Japan Times. January 06, 2016. http://www.japantimes.co.jp/community/2016/01/06/issues/japans-english-teachers-rays-hope-amid-race-bottom/.

15. "Heart English School." Glassdoor. Accessed February 29, 2016. https://www.glassdoor.com/Reviews/Heart-English-School-Reviews-E215640.htm.

16. "RCS Corporation Reviews in Japan." Glassdoor. Accessed February 29, 2016. https://www.glassdoor.co.in/Reviews/RCS-Corporation-Japan-Reviews-EI_IE25914.0,15_IL.16,21_IN123.htm.

17. "BorderLink Reviews." Glassdoor. Accessed February 29, 2016. https://www.glassdoor.com/Reviews/BorderLink-Reviews-E394975.htm.

18. "Shakai Hoken Laws Are Changing in 2016. How Will You Be Affected?" General Union. Accessed February 28, 2016. http://generalunion.org/Joomla/index.php/legal-issues/1346-shakai-hoken-laws-are-changing-in-2016-how-will-you-be-affected.

19. "General Union." Japan Visitor. Accessed February 28, 2016. http://www.japanvisitor.com/japanese-culture/language/general-union.

20. "When You Resign from a Company | 東京外国人雇用サービスセンター." Tokyo Employment Service Center for Foreigners. Accessed February 28, 2016. http://tokyo-foreigner.jsite.mhlw.go.jp/english/seekers_1/spec/spec_1d.html.

21. "Japan Visa Application Service: Application for Working Visa in Japan, Spouse Visa at an Immigration Bureau." Acroseed. Accessed

February 28, 2016. http://english.visajapan.jp/nintei.html.

22. "Entering Japan." Japan Guide. Accessed February 28, 2016. http://www.japan-guide.com/e/e2221.html.

23. "Work or Long-term Stay." Ministry of Foreign Affairs of Japan. Accessed February 28, 2016. http://www.mofa.go.jp/j_info/visit/visa/long/.

24. "JAPAN : Visa, Immigration, Working Visa, Spouse Visa." June Advisors Group. Accessed February 28, 2016. http://www.juridique.jp/immigration_bis.html.

25. "The Japan Legal / Accounting Services Visa." Japan Visa. Accessed February 28, 2016. http://www.japanvisa.com/visas/japan-legal-or-accounting-services-visa.

26. Thompson, Ashley. "Self-sponsored Visas: A Passport to Freedom or a World of Pain? | The Japan Times." Japan Times. September 04, 2012. http://www.japantimes.co.jp/community/2012/09/04/how-tos/self-sponsored-visas-a-passport-to-freedom-or-a-world-of-pain/.

27. "JAPAN : Visa, Immigration, Working Visa, Spouse Visa." June Advisors Group. Accessed February 28, 2016. http://www.juridique.jp/immigration.html.

28. "I Want to Work in Japan as a Cook." Tokyo Immigration Service. Accessed February 28, 2016. http://www.tokyoimmigration.jp/eng/ry-ouri.html.

29. "Study: Animators Earned US$28,000 on Average in Japan in 2013." Anime News Network. May 15, 2015. http://www.animenewsnetwork.com/news/2015-05-15/study-animators-earned-usd28000-on-average-in-japan-in-2013/.87762.

30. Popper, Cynthia. "Modeling in Japan: Submitting to Agents." GaijinPot. June 25, 2013. http://blog.gaijinpot.com/modeling-in-japan-submitting-to-agents/.

31. "Which Qualifications Should I Obtain to Become a Proofreader in Japan?" Yahoo! Answers. Accessed February 28, 2016. https://answers.yahoo.com/question/index?

qid=20091024010858AAhuZVG.

32. Yosomono, Eric. "7 Brutal Realities regarding Arrest in Japan." Gaijinass. January 02, 2011. http://gaijinass.com/2011/01/02/7-brutal-realities-regarding-arrest-in-japan/.

33. Debito, Arudou. "Www.debito.org: WHAT TO DO IF...quick Guide to Important Info Sites on Debito.org plus PDF Files." Debito.org. Accessed February 28, 2016. http://www.debito.org/whattodoif.html#arrested..

Printed in Poland
by Amazon Fulfillment
Poland Sp. z o.o., Wrocław